THE AUTONOMOUS BRAIN

A Neural Theory of Attention and Learning

Peter M. Milner
McGill University

LAWRENCE ERLBAUM ASSOCIATES, PUBLISHERS

1999   Mahwah, New Jersey   London

Lawrence Erlbaum Associates, Inc., Publishers
10 Industrial Avenue
Mahwah, New Jersey 07430

Library of Congress Cataloging-in-Publication Data

Milner, Peter M.
    The autonomous brain : a neural theory of attention and learning /
Peter M. Milner.
        p.   cm.
    Includes bibliographical references (p.   ) and index.
    ISBN 0-8058-3211-4 (hardcover : alk. paper)
    1. Mind and body. 2. Brain--Psychophysiology. 3. Attention.
    4. Learning, Psychology of. I. Title.
    BF161.M5 1999
    153.1--dc21   99-19772
                                                             CIP

Books published by Lawrence Erlbaum Associates are printed
on acid-free paper, and their bindings are chosen
for strength and durability.

Printed in the United States of America

10 9 8 7 6 5 4 3 2 1

Table of Contents

List of Figures

Preface

Nearly half a century ago Sperry urged what he called a motor approach to behavior, claiming that it "immediately helps us to view the brain objectively for what it is, namely, a mechanism for governing motor activity" (Sperry, 1952. P. 297). His arguments in favor of viewing perceptual activity as being closely related to the response mechanisms made a lasting impression on me, though they had little apparent effect on the direction of neuropsychological research at the time.

During the last few years, improvement in the quality and quantity of information about the motor system, and the dorsal sensory pathways that feed it, have made it easier to heed Sperry's urging. Increased interest in "thinking" robots also has tended to redress the imbalance between investigations of the output and input mechanisms of behaving organisms. For too long the observer monopolised our attention, it is time the actor took his proper place at center-stage.

The primary goal of this book is to chronicle, and perhaps hasten, the switch in emphasis from sensory systems to sensory-motor integration, but it is also intended as a tribute to Karl Lashley and Donald Hebb, two of the most creative and influential physiological psychologists of the 20th century. Both men saw clearly that the popular notion of the brain as a collection of conditionable reflexes could not begin to explain the subtleties of mammalian behavior, and both tried to find alternatives, Lashley by discounting the influence of individual neural connections, and Hebb by postulating a more complex array of connections that permitted the brain to be active independently of sensory input.

Seventy years have passed since Lashley (1929) published his monograph *Brain Mechanisms and Intelligence* and 50 since Hebb's (1949) *Organization of Behavior* appeared. Pavlovian learning theorists were not seriously shaken by Lashley's account of his failure to find specific deficits in learned behavior after brain lesions in the rat. Their response was to deny the value of brain research for psychological theory. Nevertheless, Lashley's data were frequently cited by neurologists opposed to the theory of cerebral localization.

Hebb's primary message that feedback connections provide the brain with endogenous sources of activity also was ignored for a number of years by learning theorists, whereas his postulates concerning the mechanism of synaptic change were adopted by connectionist modelers (mostly of stimulus-response theories) and neurophysiologists.

Both Lashley and Hebb tackled interesting and difficult problems that other psychologists were inclined to bypass, but their quests for neural mechanisms were often led astray by lack of reliable neurophysiological information. During the past half century, the face of biology has changed completely, especially in the areas of genetics and neuroscience. Although some investigators (typical examples are Robert Desimone, Joachim Fuster, J. H. R. Maunsell and Wolf Singer) have made it clear that their research is relevant to important psychological problems, somewhat to my surprise, the implication of their work does not seem to have been widely recognized by nonphysiological psychologists, and psychological theory has been slow to react to these developments.

Some of the questions raised by Lashley and Hebb have intrigued me for a long time, and several years ago I decided that advances in neuroscience made renewed attempts to answer them worthwhile. How are ideas represented in the brain? How do they become associated with responses and with each other? How are all the patterns of retinal stimulation that result from observing the different exemplars of a category interpreted by the brain as being in some sense equivalent?

The latter riddle was posed by Lashley to confound stimulus - response learning theorists. Lashley also pondered the mystery of how the brain stores and uses information about temporal sequences, an important feature of real-world stimuli that still receives less attention than it deserves. The focus exhibited by most behavior raises the broad issue of selective attention, which only recently has become a topic of interest to neuroscientists.

Satisfactory neural explanations for these phenomena and many others were impossible to achieve before about 1950 because most people believed that synaptic transmission was electrical and very brief. Recognition of the chemical nature of synaptic transmission and the subsequent discoveries of the complicated and lengthy chemical changes that occur during neural activity had little effect on psychological theory for a long time. Indeed, synaptic transmission still is assumed to have the characteristics of an electrical impulse in many contemporary neural network models.

Currently, however, behavioral neuroscientists are likely to know as much about the neuron as the average physiologist, if not more. But they are usually too interested in the pharmacological or anatomical details of the system under investigation to devote much thought to the question of how their research might influence the big picture.

Ideas and attitudes of a former era linger and, in my view, interfere with clear thinking about important psychological issues. Since the early days of philosophy, there has been persistent bickering concerning the relative contributions of learning and inheritance to behavior. The first behaviorists adopted an extreme empiricist position as an antidote to vitalism, a doctrine in vogue at the time (Driesch, 1908), and for a variety of reasons, most psychologists to this day are more inclined than other biologists to attribute behavior to learning. This is particularly apparent in neural network modeling, whose exponents usually try to start with an absolute minimum of organized structure.

The high degree of anatomical stereotypy, at both the microscopic and macroscopic levels of the brain strongly suggest that psychologists tend to underestimate the influence of innate factors on behavior. In this treatise the explanations of neural mechanisms are based on the assumption that a great many basic circuits are genetically designed for the purposes they serve. Only when the effective functioning of a neural structure requires information that could not be inherited, is learning invoked. The assumption more commonly adopted by behaviorists, that a mechanism is learned unless it can be proved otherwise, is guaranteed to be misleading because genetic adaptation is, in fact, just a very long-drawn-out process of trial-and-error learning.

Perhaps the most conspicuous discrepancy between behaviorist theories and common sense concerns the self-concept. I imagine all sane and sober people have the feeling that they personally exert considerable control over their important actions. An entity we call the self makes plans, and chooses when to embark on them. For most of the 20th century, classical psychological theory has frowned on the idea that behavior depends on anything but the impinging stimuli and the learned aftereffects of previous stimulation. Any intervention by an ego or other so-called mental process was considered a step on the slippery slope to vitalism.

I believe this discrepancy is now resolved, or is well on the way toward resolution. Increasingly it is recognized that the self does not need to be outside the body; it may more conveniently be thought of as a complex neural mechanism, often referred to as the brain's executive system. In the view of many, including me, the self has a predominantly genetic basis. Observations of brain activity suggest that a central process, closely related to motivational and response mechanisms, is responsible for selecting responses and determining what sensory input is required to execute them. This central process makes use of the strong reciprocal paths through the sensory systems to highlight the relevant input. No doubt this is the autonomous system that gives us the feeling that we are in control of our destiny. It is the basis for the title of this book.

A related problem concerns the directedness of our trains of thought. Most psychologists now accept that concepts form associations with each other and attribute this to potentiation of synapses linking the neural representations of the concepts. Occasionally someone raises the question of what sort of wiring would be needed to ensure that every concept has the possibility of instantly associating with every other concept, but the question is soon set aside. After all, concepts do become associated with each other. Or do they?

Another problem is that concepts do not have just one association. Most have hundreds but they come to mind only one at a time. And not just any association at random, usually it is a relevant one. This is not a fortunate accident. The thinker, be it a person or some other animal, has learned what stimuli are required or useful in a certain situation, so associations stem not only from the sensory input but also, and perhaps more importantly, from the central executive system.

The stimulus - response model has penetrated the 20th century psyche to the

PREFACE

core. It is time to contemplate the contrary idea that responses become associated with stimuli that can bring fulfilment. Hence it is an intention that often determines which association of a concept is implemented. A main theme of this monograph is that response - stimulus learning has an important bearing on the question of how concepts are associated with each other.

Many people have contributed to this work, most of them unwittingly through reports of their research. My colleagues at McGill University have been very supportive, providing encouragement and frequent consultation during the rather protracted gestation. Brenda Milner of the Montreal Neurological Institute kept me informed of developments in many areas related to memory. During the early stages of the writing, and when I began to fear that I would never find a plausible explanation for the association of ideas, I enjoyed a voluminous and somewhat philosophical exchange of correspondence with Seth Sharpless, then at the University of Colorado, and a friend since we were graduate students of Donald Hebb together.

Donald Hebb died in 1985, but he deserves special acknowledgment because it was his book, *The Organization of Behavior,* that started it all by drawing me into psychology from a war-time career in electronic and nuclear engineering. Rod Cooper, a somewhat more recent student of Hebb, has read most of the manuscript at various stages of its evolution, and was even enthusiastic (or rash) enough to use some of it in an undergraduate course at the University of Calgary. My wife, Susan, worked valiantly to keep me in touch with the world outside the brain.

I should like also to thank the Lawrence Erlbaum Associates team for their cheerful assistance in the production of this book, especially Susan Milmoe whose editorial encouragement and advice led to a great improvement of the manuscript.

Peter M. Milner

Montreal
April 1999.

1 Introduction

WHERE TO START?

How does anyone set about trying to discover how the brain regulates behavior? Dismantling it, the traditional approach of budding scientists to alarm clocks (in the days when alarm clocks were full of clockwork), may reveal how it looks, but not how it works. There is no-one to whom the investigator can write for a manual or a blueprint. Confronted by billions of cells connected by untold miles of threadlike processes, early psychologists were inclined to give up on the problem and concentrate on making sense of the behavior it produced.

About half a century ago improved techniques of staining made it possible to follow many of the brain's connections. At about the same time, the microstructure of neurons and their electrophysiological and chemical properties began to be investigated more thoroughly. As knowledge about the nervous system grew, the possibility of discovering how it works began to seem less remote. Also more worthwhile, because the knowledge could be applied to a greater body of neural information to explain behavior and its impairments.

Anyone who has looked at the circuit diagram of a moderately complicated piece of electronic equipment, or the printout of a computer program, in the hope of discovering its purpose, will realize the hopelessness of trying to figure out what sort of behavior the brain will produce simply by studying its connections and the properties of the component neurons. Even knowing the purpose of the equipment, and exactly how all the components work, does not make it easy to relate structure to function in a complex system (Braitenberg, 1984).

Fortunately, in the case of the brain, we would be satisfied to discover just the general principles of how it produces the behavior that we can observe. A close analogy is seen in the inventor, who knows the purpose of his invention and has to think of a good way of assembling it from the parts available. Knowing something about the structure of the brain can help, but by far the most useful information relates to the behavior it produces. In any case, it is easier to observe behavior than brain activity, and we know a great deal more about it. Therefore, basing our theories of brain function on a knowledge of behavior would seem to be more sensible than trying to do the opposite.

Despite its reasonableness, this precept is not often strictly followed. After all, the brain, though not very accessible, is made of real stuff; behavior is insubstantial. Pavlov (1927), following Sechenov (1863/1965), made the mistake of starting with the spinal reflex, a physiological mechanism he knew something about, and letting it dictate his concept of behavior. The behavior on which he based his theory of learning was that of dogs responding in a quite atypical and artificial situation.

Lashley (1950), whose life also was devoted to the problem of brain and behavior, concluded early in his career that brain processes must be very diffuse, believing that individual neurons and their connections have little influence on behavior. Lashley also had a long-standing prejudice against attributing learning to synaptic change. To some extent, these attitudes about brain processes colored his perception of behavior (Lashley, 1924).

A third major contributor to neural theories of behavior, Hebb (1949, 1980), took the anatomical findings of Lorente de Nó (1938) as the inspiration for his cell assembly concept. Although he was a strong advocate for basing neuropsychological theory on behavioral evidence, he frequently interpreted behavioral data in terms of his anatomically inspired model of brain function.

Once the behavior to be explained or simulated has been thoroughly studied, the design of a model may be implemented in various ways. It is possible, for example, to use electronic components to construct a machine that locates sources of energy and recharges itself, mimicking the appetitive behavior of a simple animal. A working model is very convincing, but there are advantages in conceiving a hypothetical model based on components as similar as possible to those found in the nervous system. In the first place, such a model allows the correspondence between the design and the real thing to be assessed more directly. Also, if it proves necessary to postulate hitherto unknown physiological mechanisms to account for certain behaviors, the hypothetical model makes it possible to seek confirmation in the real nervous system.

WHY DID THE CHICKEN CROSS THE ROAD?

An important theme of this monograph is that behavior is not always determined by sensory stimulation. Of course, this is not a new discovery. Behavioral autonomy is something most people throughout the ages have taken to be self-evident. Many still do, but they typically attribute their autonomy, not to a material brain, but to an incorporeal ego, or "self," that imbues the body with life and purpose.

This attribution had an unfortunate consequence. When psychologists towards the end of the 19th century began to question the notion that a physical body can be controlled by a disembodied spirit, they also doubted, or more likely did not even consider, the possibility that the body itself might possess the means to initiate behavior. They assumed the body to be inert except when activated by sensory input.

Nevertheless, as any electronics engineer will testify, complicated material structures readily make use of whatever energy is accessible to generate unexpected (and usually undesired) output. Few mechanisms can equal the complexity of the mammalian nervous system. It is a scene of literally billions of interrelated chemical reactions. Newborn infants, when awake, usually find some way of making their presence known. The more impoverished the external stimulation, the more vigorous their efforts are likely to become (at least in the short term).

Lashley (1951), and Hebb (1949, p. 3) were among those who criticized the reflex model, in which behavior is attributed entirely to sensory input. Hebb did not believe the internal influences on behavior to be innate, however. His view was that they develop as a result of previous stimulation. In any case, the criticisms of these researchers had negligible effect. The notion that behavior is always a reaction to a stimulus is so ingrained that the name applied by psychologists to an element of behavior is "response."

PERCEPTION, INTENTION, AND ATTENTION

The possibility that the nervous system may generate responses independently of sensory input has important implications for the way we view sensory mechanisms. Because typical neural theories of behavior depict the nervous system as a device that processes sensory input to derive adaptive responses from it, perception and memory are given priority treatment. Often, response mechanisms are ignored or taken for granted.

It is hardly surprising, therefore, that theories and research aimed specifically at explaining perception and recognition are typically based on the assumption that these processes can be studied in isolation, with little if any reference to activity in other parts of the brain. Theories of recognition, for example, concentrate on the creation of memory traces and their relation to subsequent sensory input. Until recently (Desimone & Duncan, 1995; Rizzolatti, Riggio, & Sheliga, 1994), account was rarely taken of the fact that our motivation and actions have a decisive

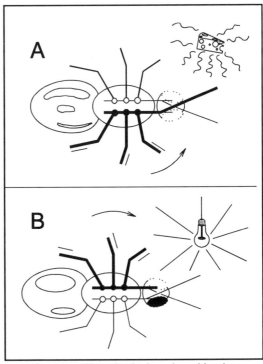

FIG. 1.1.   Hypothetical goal-seeking bug.

impact on what we perceive, though Sperry (1952) long ago pointed out that the sensory systems evolved to improve the performance of the motor system, not the reverse.

The problem is exemplified by the dilemma of the goal-seeking bug shown in Fig. 1.1 (Milner, 1970). An odor to the left of the bug energizes predominantly its right legs, turning the creature toward the olfactory stimulus. Light falling on the bug's left eye energizes predominantly its left legs, turning it away from the light. But what happens if the bug is confronted by a floodlit plate of food? Or worse, suppose the food is in front and a light to one side? With two sources of sensory input trying to steer the bug in different directions, it would never reach the food, nor would it run directly away from the light. To function effectively, the bug must be able to ignore all stimuli except the one it considers most important.

This sort of dilemma is not a freak accident. It happens all the time. On a summer evening, a hunting bat may receive sonar echoes from dozens of flying objects, but it must "lock on" to only one of them at a time if it is to catch anything. In the presence of several stimuli, animals may be forced to choose between possible courses of action and, having decided on one, they must prevent any irrelevant input from interfering with the behavior.

It might said that animals focus their attention on the object they most urgently need. If that object is not present, they may settle for one of lower priority. A very hungry and less thirsty animal would be able to drink if food were absent because, although the sensory path for food may be more strongly sensitized than that for water, the facilitation is ineffective when there is no food.

Theorists often pay lip service to the influence of attention on perception (the word "attention" here, as elsewhere throughout the book, means *selective* attention, a process that highlights a particular stimulus), but they rarely, if ever, incorporate attention into their theories in a formal or useful way. Attention admittedly is difficult to incorporate into neural models of perception because it involves taking account of the animal's intentions. Although in experiments, stimuli can be controlled very precisely, determining an animal's intention is more difficult.

Nineteenth century introspectionists such as Külpe (1901) speculated at length about the influence of intention on all aspects of behavior, but intention had no place in the behaviorists' reflex-based theory. In that theory, responses were supposed to depend only on stimuli, certainly not on mental concepts such as intention. The pioneer behaviorists would have found the possibility that planning a response could induce profound changes in the sensory systems, as demonstrated by Moran and Desimone (1985) for example, too unsettling even to contemplate.

The new wave of conditioning theorists, including Mackintosh (1975), Rescorla and Wagner (1972), and especially Grossberg (1975), attempting to explain the results of Kamin's (1969) "blocking" experiments, recognized the relation between motivation and attention. However, any influence this might have had on neural theories of perception has been slow to make itself felt.

More recently, Rizzolatti (1983) has speculated along similar lines. On the basis of results from single-unit recordings in cats and lesions in monkeys and human patients, he argues that attention is not a centralized sensory process that can be directed at will to enhance any stimulus, but that it consists of the facilitation of sensory neurons by premotor activity during the preparation for a response.

The evidence supports this view with respect to attention directed to a point in space, but for a response that is to be directed to a particular object, Rizzolatti provides no convincing answer to the problem of how the premotor activity locates sensory neurons that represent that object. R. Miller and Wickens (1991), in discussing their version of the cell assembly theory, also stress the importance of selective attention. They note the relation of attention to the motor system, but do not develop its role in the execution of responses. This problem was raised some time ago (Milner, 1974) and is discussed at greater length in chapter 4.

Most investigators of perception concentrate on sensory input and its aftereffects, paying less regard than does Rizzolatti to contributions from the response system. This has led to a number of problems that will subsequently be discussed.

One obvious problem is that almost everything we see or hear has innumerable potential associations, only one of which is aroused at any time. Not only does attention select the items relevant to the current task from the vast array of sensory input, it also determines which associations of those items should be followed up. It is obvious, and frequently noted, that attention focuses on one or other feature in the sensory field, but few investigators have attempted to explain how it identifies and targets the relevant stimuli.

One theme of the present thesis is that sensitization of the appropriate sensory pathways is an essential component of any response. The urge to perform some act comes first, exerting a major influence on the type of stimulus to which the sensory system is attuned. Of course, emergency signals can break through to change the animal's motivation, but such is not the normal course of events. Investigators of perceptual mechanisms disregard this at their peril.

STIMULI AS INITIATORS OR GUIDES

Although the theory advanced in this discussion lays stress on the primacy of the motor system, undoubtedly animals often embark on activities as a result of a stimulus, either internal or external. If an animal is cold, for example, it will seek some way of warming itself; effects of sex hormones determine the priority assigned to the search for a mate. The smell of a favorite food may entice an animal to eat, even when it is not sufficiently hungry to forage for food. Once a goal has been established, however, attention is focused on stimuli needed to proceed with the task. The cold animal, for example, may have learned where shelter is located, and attends mainly to "signposts" along the route to make its way there.

Thus stimuli are seen to play a dual function in this model, serving sometimes to motivate, and at other times to inform and guide responses. Classical learning theory, because of its lack of interest in the details of responding, frequently merged these two functions. A trained rat was assumed to approach and press a Skinner-box lever because of an association between the lever and that response. This assumption ignores the fact that the Skinner box presents many stimuli, any of which might control the rat's behavior. The fact that the rat fixes on the visual input from the lever to guide its approach indicates that it already had a plan, possibly before it even entered the box, in which the lever featured as an object of attention.

The response-centered learning theory presented here is more in keeping with an animal's behavior. It postulates that bar-pressing is one of a number of responses an experienced laboratory rat has associated with food. The onset of a plan to eat facilitates neurons that have become associated with food in different contexts such as the home cage, a Skinner box, or the goal box of a maze. If a stimulus related to food is present in the sensory field of a hungry rat, it biases a response selection mechanism in favor of the plan that is most consistent with the perceived situation (approaching a lever in the presence of Skinner-box stimuli or perhaps approaching an experimenter whose lunch it occasionally shares).

The plan, once it takes effect, focuses attention on stimuli required for an initial response, thus ensuring that the response is directed to the intended target. According to this theory, a food-deprived rat well-versed in laboratory routine associates the experimenter's approach to its home cage with being fed. The motivation to eat, thus aroused, initiates a plan to approach and press a Skinner-box lever.

Obviously, the plan cannot be put into effect until the rat has identified and located the lever, and that requires attention. In this example, the stimulus that establishes the intention (the approach of the experimenter) is quite different from the stimulus to which the plan of the intended response directs attention (the lever).

THE EVOLUTION OF BEHAVIOR

The ultimate goal of psychology is to explain human behavior, in which learning plays a major part. We should recognize, however, that learning is a relatively recent evolutionary development, and that most of the animal population, including some of the most successful species, flourish with negligible capacity for individual learning. Some build snares, for example, or communal dwellings that would tax the ingenuity and skill of a human. They prepare food and shelter for offspring they will never see.

Depending on whether an animal is hungry, in pursuit of a mate, or in search of a place to lay its eggs, different patterns of sensory-motor integration are brought into play. For the purpose of reproduction, a drastic change of gene regulation rebuilds not only the nervous system, but the whole body of typical insects. Their astonishingly complex and diverse behavior results almost entirely from the inherent structure (and restructuring) of their nervous systems.

Insects and other small organisms usually are prolific, which allows the species to adapt to environmental changes by the selection of individuals accidentally equipped to survive them. Larger, less prolific animals have evolved a more individualistic method of coping with unfriendly environments: They learn.

Learning is not a substitute for innate behavior; it is an example of it. Learning is an evolutionary development that allows fine tuning of a very complex piece of predominantly heritable machinery (Lashley, 1947; Tinbergen, 1951). It is foolish to hope to understand the behavior of higher animals such as primates, while remaining ignorant of the instinctive mechanisms that are only partially, and often with great difficulty, modified by learned adaptations. Consequently, before tackling the more difficult problems that arise when innate behavior is augmented by learning it is helpful to try to understand the behavior of animals that can learn very little,.

Basic survival demands that animals recognize sources of nourishment and dangerous situations, and respond accordingly by approaching the former and evading the latter. Animals that learn can transfer the motivational properties of innately reinforcing stimuli to accompanying or perceptibly related stimuli. Thus, the sight of a food dish acquires the ability to attract an animal that was previously attracted only by the smell of the food it contained. What is transferred in this example is the tendency to approach, not a particular set of movements. A dog may never have jumped for food, certainly never in the presence of its food dish, nevertheless it will jump on a chair if that is where the dish has been placed.

An animal also will show excitement, and salivate, when it sees its food dish. In fact, it behaves in many ways as if the dish were the food. For that reason the animal often is said to *expect* food when it sees the dish, although that is an inference based on our own introspection. Just as animals innately become sensitive to the smell of food when hungry, hunger also causes animals to attend to stimuli that have acquired an association with food.

In other words, attention initially directed only to an innate reinforcer is, after learning, directed to objects associated with the reinforcer. It is important to observe that learning not only allows initially neutral objects to arouse a motivational state, it also links the motivation system to perceptual systems via pathways that must run in a direction opposite to the conventional sensory paths.

This is an important aspect of response learning still generally ignored, even though it was proposed almost a quarter of a century ago by Grossberg (1975) to explain problems of Pavlovian conditioning, and by P. M. Milner (1974) to explain problems arising in visual perception. It is discussed more fully in later chapters.

NEURAL REPRESENTATION OF STIMULI

An animal in need of nourishment becomes sensitive to stimuli that indicate the presence of food, and is guided by them. According to the model outlined earlier, the motivational system facilitates neurons that process input from receptors stimulated by food, ensuring that those neurons gain control of the locomotor system when food is in the vicinity. If the animal is dehydrated, different neurons become active in the motivational system and facilitate sensory neurons that are stimulated by stimuli from water. In this way, water-sensitive neurons gain control of the locomotor mechanism and block any conflicting stimuli that might interfere with the animal's approach to water.

In animals that are innately attracted by a satisfier such as a particular food, neurons in the motivation system must be "hard-wired" to sensory neurons that represent the satisfier. Thus neurons whose activity indicates the presence of food, water, or a dangerous predator must all be determined innately, so that they may be identified and facilitated by neurons carrying selective attention signals from the corresponding need systems.

How then are the sensory systems organized so that the receptors stimulated by a particular object fire neurons that can be innately recognized by a corresponding motivational activity? It is easy to see how neurons whose activity represents a particular olfactory stimulus might be connected to their receptors. In the simplest case, a receptor is sensitive to only one stimulus, such as the smell of water vapor, so they may be connected directly to neurons representing the presence of water. For more complex odors that require stimulation of combinations of receptors, convergence of signals from those receptors on neurons representing the odor achieves a similar effect.

Much the same arrangement of connections provides for the innate neural representation of movement, colors, or sound frequencies, but complications arise in representing visual shapes. Detection of a shape requires the cooperation of many receptors. Whereas a given smell always stimulates the same group of olfactory receptors, a given shape rarely stimulates the same group of light receptors. This could happen only if the shape projected an image of constant size, orientation, and location in the visual field. As further discussed in chapter 4, special circuits are required to derive neural representations corresponding to shapes.

The neural representation of stimuli that critically depend on a temporal sequence, as is true for many sounds, poses an equally challenging problem. In such cases, the representation of the stimulus must involve some way of representing order. The processing and storage of temporal order also enters into the generation of almost all responses. Possible mechanisms are discussed in chapter 5.

So far, we have considered only the situation in which the motivational system is innately connected to neurons representing significant inputs, but as was mentioned in the previous section, animals that can learn must be able to focus their attention on any arbitrary stimulus that happens to appear regularly in conjunction with a basic reinforcer. Mechanisms for establishing new connections between motivational and perceptual elements are described in chapters 4 and 9.

SUMMARY

The idea that a true understanding of behavior must take the nervous system into account has gained ground during the half century since Hebb's (1949) *Organization of Behavior* was published, but the centuries-old spinal reflex analogy still constitutes an impediment to this goal.

When Descartes (1662/1955) introduced the reflex explanation of behavior, he augmented it with a link (via the pineal gland) to an autonomous soul. The behaviorists severed this link about a century ago without providing any replacement. My aim in this work is to show how innate motivational and response systems of the brain frequently generate behavior independently of sensory input.

In the proposed model, perception is strongly influenced by what the organism is planning to do, implying important pathways from the response system to the sensory systems. Effective responding requires precise filtering of sensory input so that only relevant stimuli are applied to the task. In animals that learn, modification of these reciprocal pathways is of major importance. Thus motivation can be directed to initially nonreinforcing objects.

2 The Behavior Model

If behavior is to be used to throw light on the nervous system, it is important to have a model that effectively summarizes the behavior we hope to explain. Although it is possible to quibble about the terminology, natural selection may be regarded as the first, and most basic learning mechanism. Almost all the marvelously adaptive behavior of arthropods, and much of that seen in vertebrates, is acquired by random genetic variability and selection. The ability of individuals to augment their innate capabilities as a result of personal experience is a bonus. It is clear that we must try to understand the behavior of the basic automaton before speculating on how it is modified by individual learning (Vanderwolf, 1998; Vanderwolf & Cain, 1994).

INNATE GOAL SEEKING

The main advantage that most animals have over other forms of life is that they can move about, enabling them to approach things they need and escape from threatening situations. Inanimate goal-seeking automata, using error-reducing feedback, have been around for many years. Grey Walter's *machina speculatrix* (Walter, 1953) used this principle to approach a faint light; Braitenberg's book *"Vehicles"* (1984) contains designs for goal-seeking machines of greater complexity. The hypothetical goal-switching bug described in chapter 1 (Fig. 1.1), operates on the same principle.

The ability to switch tasks is almost universal among animals. Survival, at its most basic, involves replenishing sources of energy and escaping from harmful situations. Depending on the goal, different stimuli engage the approach mechanism to control the direction of locomotion. A crucial component of every animal's behavior is the ability to select the stimulus for locomotor guidance most appropriate to the situation in which it finds itself.

Some of the simpler molluscs and arthropods, whose capacity to learn is quite limited, nevertheless undertake elaborate construction projects and courtship ceremonies. Innate performances such as these demand singleness of purpose and must be regulated by specific stimuli. Intrusion of extraneous movements, elicited by stray stimuli, might well prove fatal.

A dragonfly, for instance, needs a stretch of water in which to lay its eggs. Once detected, the location of the water relative to the insect determines the flight path and release of the eggs. Sensory input from the water surface alone, with all other sensory input suppressed, is essential for the success of the mission. In general, of all the numerous stimuli surrounding an animal, only one, prescribed by the goal selector, is admitted to the motor system to guide its activity.

CHOOSING THE RIGHT STIMULUS

In chapter 1, it was suggested that the stimuli required for goal-directed performances are selected by attention, which also blocks the influence of irrelevant sensory input on the motor system. The origin of attention was postulated to be the intended performance (i.e., whatever the animal decides to do in a given situation).

Obviously the decision process is at the heart of behavior. Subjectively, it is an action of the "self," but animals not usually suspected of having self-awareness also make decisions. However strongly we believe a fly to be an automaton, lacking consciousness and at the mercy of its instincts, when we see it buzzing around and finally alighting on our sandwich, it is hard to suppress the impression that it is the deliberate action of a sentient being. (An ill-advised action, perhaps, but freely chosen.) The neural circuits that accomplish the choosing evolved, as did the wings, eyes, and other statistically improbable appurtenances, because they improve the fly's chances of survival and reproduction.

The decisions arrived at by the selection mechanism may not always appear rational, but we must assume that they are always based on the data available at the time, data derived from the history of the species, modified by any more recent genetic accidents that may have occurred, and, in the case of animals that can learn, by any relevant information the individual has absorbed along the way.

At the center of our model, then, we must imagine a goal selector (Fig. 2.1) with inputs from detectors of needs (usually internal stimuli) and satisfiers of the needs (external stimuli), often called reinforcers. The goal selector has evolved to activate responses that, in the animal's natural environment, are most likely to reduce the need.

The important question, of course, concerns the mechanism by which one of the possible responses is chosen. A few "automatic" responses can continue in the background without interfering with other responses, but for the most part only one response plan controls the motor system at any time. This suggests that most of the potential response plans inhibit each other. The one with the most facilitation (or the least inhibition) "wins" and suppresses the rest. The response selector is energized by input from a subcortical arousal system that is active during waking and rapid-eye-movement sleep (Llinas & Ribary, 1993). Thus, even when sensory input is at a low level, response planning may continue.

As it facilitates (or "primes") the motor components of the selected response, the goal selector also switches attention to the sensory input necessary for effective responding. In fact, the response system may elicit some actions indirectly by facilitating sensory input that innately releases them.

Unattended signals not immediately necessary for the performance of a response may also be processed by the sensory systems and delivered to the goal selector to help determine future responses. These stimuli are, however, excluded from the parts of the motor system engaged in performing the selected task. It is important for any model of behavior to distinguish these two roles of sensory input: that of participating in the competition with other neural activities to select a response, and that of guiding any response thereby selected.

Sometimes the initiating and response-directing stimuli are the same, although different aspects may be involved. A frog, for example, may be put into a feeding mode by movement of a small object anywhere in its visual field, but the trajectory of its predatory tongue flick is determined by the location of the moving spot on its retina.

For some tasks the goal-setting stimulus may be olfactory, and the goal-targeting stimulus visual or auditory. In animals that do not learn, only innately motivating stimuli can influence the goal selector or, to put it another way, stimuli that influence the choice between different modes of behavior are classed as motivators or reinforcers. A very large class of stimuli elicits avoidance in most animals. It includes vibration, noise, tastes and smells (other than those of necessities such as food, water, and mates), and almost anything large that moves.

A GOAL-SELECTING MODEL

Figure 2.1 diagrams a simple model of a non-learning organism that can satisfy a few typical needs. The diagram shows a goal selector that receives input from external and internal sources. The internal signals provide information about the state

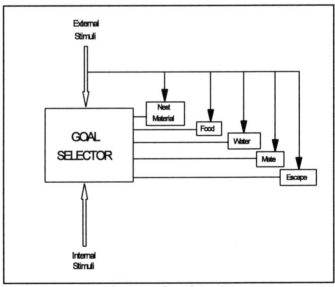

FIG. 2.1.   Goal Selection.

of the animal, whilst the animal's sense organs provide information about the environment.

2   As mentioned earlier, the information is assessed by the goal selector to determine which, if any, of the animal's innate goal-related mechanisms should be deployed. If none of the external stimuli elicits an innate response, and if the organism is not in a resting state, it moves about at random, improving its chances of encountering something it needs. As this automaton cannot learn, it neither avoids places it has explored already , nor does it find its way more quickly to a previously rewarded place.

Figure 2.2 is a diagram showing one of the postulated innate response generators, the one that subserves feeding. When the organism is hungry and detects a smell of food, the output of the goal selector admits only food-related stimuli to control approach behavior.

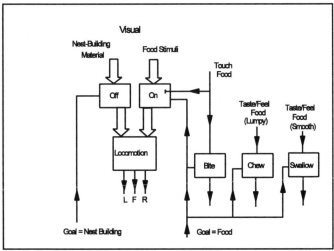

FIG. 2.2.   Innate approach and feeding systems.

The figure also depicts a subsystem for controlling approach to nest-building materials, but this subsystem receives no enabling input from the goal selector when food is the chosen goal. In this case, its signals do not reach the locomotor system and have no effect on it.

As in the case of the bug described earlier, if the stimuli from food are strongest on the left, they produce more vigorous movements of the right (R) legs (or other propellants) and vice versa, turning the organism toward the source of the stimulation. When the stimulation is equal on both sides, the model moves straight forward (F). In that way it should eventually reach the food. If the nesting-material path had been activated instead of the food path, the animal would have approached nest-building material, using different input stimuli applied to the same approach mechanism.

When food is the goal, the output of the goal selector also primes innate motor systems for biting, chewing, and swallowing. Although these functions are illustrated as distinct modules or boxes in Fig. 2.2, this is for clarity only; anatomically they overlap. Aided by the attentional facilitation, contact with the food releases biting (in this particular hypothetical organism) and inhibits locomotion. Then tactual and taste stimuli from food in the mouth evoke chewing, and when the tactual stimuli indicate that the food is reduced to sufficiently small pieces, swallowing is released. As food is ingested, the hunger input to the goal selector diminishes, and when it falls below threshold, feeding stops. Food then may be replaced by some other goal.

During eating, the goal selector continues to receive information about the internal state of the organism and the presence of objects in the world outside. If a motivating stimulus of higher priority, such as the smell of a predator, is experienced, the goal selector switches tasks. The approach to food is aborted and a response to the more urgent stimulus is initiated.

Some responses, such as escape from contact (especially painful contact), loud noises, and (in photophobic species) light, command a high priority and are continuously ready to be released. The sensitivity of other response plans to their initiating stimuli fluctuates under the control of circadian clocks, sexual cycles, and other internal states.

Thus, certain genetically determined stimuli have constant access to the goal-selecting mechanism whereas stimuli needed to guide the performance gain access to the motor system only when a path is made available by appropriate activity of the response selector.

EXPLORING AND LEARNING

The previous section described how a "pure" robot might maintain itself in a suitable environment, but it is not likely that any real animals are completely without memory. Almost all neural communication is chemical, and most chemical processes produce persistent aftereffects. Memory mechanisms have evolved to make use of some of these chemical aftereffects. The ability of animals to remember how they coped with past needs and emergencies, improves their chances of surviving subsequent crises. Most animals can, at least, learn their local topography.

Enabling animals to operate in the presence of harmless stimuli is an almost universal function of learning. Most animals innately avoid objects they have not previously encountered. Unfamiliar objects may be dangerous, treating them with caution has survival value. If persisted in, however, such circumspect behavior could interfere with feeding and other necessary activities to the extent that the benefit of prudence would be lost. A tortoise that withdraws into its shell at every puff of wind or whenever a cloud casts a shadow would never win races, not even with a lazy hare.

To overcome this problem, almost all animals habituate to benign stimuli that occur frequently. Confronted by a strange object, a naive animal may freeze or attempt to hide, but if nothing unpleasant happens, sooner or later it will resume its activity. The possibility also exists that an unfamiliar object may be useful, so if it poses no immediate threat, a closer inspection may be worthwhile.

Thus, a bipolar response to novelty is common. In a totally unfamiliar situation, animals respond as they do to an innately recognized danger signal. As the situation becomes somewhat more familiar, however, the fear or vigilance is attenuated by habituation, releasing an underlying attraction to mystery objects, also innate.

Apart from the fact that exploration has no lasting value unless the explorer can learn, an exploring non-learner would soon wear itself out by continually avoiding or investigating useless stimuli. Being unable to stop investigating useless objects is worse than being persistently afraid of them. These adaptive reactions to novel stimuli are of use only to animals that habituate. To others they would constitute fatal traps. Learning makes possible the habituation of both fear and curiosity. These characteristics must have evolved in parallel.

REINFORCEMENT OF LEARNED BEHAVIOR

If, at any time, the investigation of an unfamiliar stimulus uncovers a reinforcer (i.e., an innately significant stimulus), something quite different happens. The sensory input from the unfamiliar stimulus acquires connections with the emotions and response plans elicited by the reinforcer. A strange object that on closer inspection smells of a dangerous predator or delivers an electric shock acquires an association with the escape and fear responses provoked by those stimuli.

A strange object that is found to have an appetizing smell or taste acquires associations with approach, salivation, and other preliminaries to feeding. No simple learning formula can resolve the paradox that the fear induced by unfamiliar objects declines without spreading to associated objects whereas fear induced by some aspect of an injurious object is readily associated with contiguous events and other aspects of the object. Presumably, these outcomes result from distinct mechanisms that evolved because of their survival value. An animal that habituated too readily to damaging stimuli, or never habituated to innocuous ones, would have diminished opportunity to pass on its genes.

In the Pavlovian conditioning situation, a stimulus repeatedly presented before food or a shock elicits many of the responses innately evoked by the reinforcing stimulus. For example, pigeons fed grain shortly after a light is turned on eventually start pecking at the light. If the onset of light is followed by water instead of grain, their pecking of the light is noticeably different, resembling more closely a drinking response than a feeding peck (Jenkins & Moore, 1973).

Racoons rewarded by food for depositing a token in a piggy bank, start rubbing the tokens together, as they normally treat their food when washing it (Breland & Breland, 1961). An innate reinforcer, if present, almost always dominates any new stimulus to which the animal has acquired an attachment, so that when food is detected, for example, it is preferred to a Skinner-box lever.

We see that spontaneous activity, itself an innate disposition, is important for learning, and must be taken into account in any behavior model. Exploration may occur in the absence of any reinforcing stimulus, but it need no longer be random when the animal can learn. Our hypothetical organism can now remember where it has been and either avoid returning, if nothing of interest was there, or go there again if it found a reward. Of course, a place where something frightening occurred is avoided more promptly and persistently than a place where nothing happens.

Suppose that the response system of our simple learner has, like that of the robot in Fig. 2.1, a repertoire of innately programmed activities, one of which is to approach and investigate stimuli that are unknown but not threatening. If there are several such objects, the exploration mechanism is assumed to employ a "winner takes all" strategy similar to the one proposed to select innate responses in the non-learning automaton described earlier. Only one stimulus at a time can be the target for investigation.

A simple neural model that could explain habituation would, like the *Aplysia* (Castellucci & Kandel, 1974), have synapses to the motor system that undergo long-term depression. Their effectiveness would be reduced for a time after use. Thus, after a stimulus has been approached and examined several times, its effect on the approach system weakens, and some other stimulus might assume the dominant guiding role. A succession of stimuli might be explored in this way, each one in turn losing its grip on the approach mechanism. Finally, no stimulus would effectively capture the locomotor system, and another activity such as vocalizing, digging, or sleeping, might become dominant.

ACQUIRED MOTIVATION

This simple model of habituation does not adequately describe the behavior of higher animals. For them, the evidence suggests that the occurrence of a response depends on its predicted outcome. An animal may repeatedly perform a response whose outcome is unpredictable, even if none of the outcomes is of immediate value. Monkeys work to be able to watch a toy train running round a track, for example, or to catch glimpses of people working in an adjacent room (Butler, 1953). People persistently watch television or put coins into gambling machines.

A more elaborate model is needed to explain outcome-dependent habituation and motivation. Its specifications might read as follows:

- If the intention to make a response in a particular situation elicits no prediction of what the outcome may be, the response is not inhibited.

- It is inhibited, however, if in the light of previous experience its outcome can be predicted as unreinforcing.

- If the predicted outcome is a reward, then the intended response is facilitated.

- If an aversive outcome is predicted, the response is strongly inhibited.

In other words, the fate of a response being planned depends on the motivational nature of the associations aroused by the plan. A response that has boring associations is eventually inhibited. Responses that have painful associations are inhibited more rapidly and strongly. Responses that have associations with reward are facilitated (or released from inhibition) in proportion to the attractiveness of their predicted outcome.

The context of the response is, of course, an important factor in predicting its expected outcome. The response plan and the current sensory input are combined in a sensory-motor analyzer (Fig. 2.3) to provide a signal that has previously been associated with the motivational effect of the outcome.

Figure 2.3 is a diagram of a response mechanism that conforms to the preceding specifications. Neurons of an analyzer fired by the combined response plan and sensory input deliver a signal to a motivation system that, on the basis of associations made with the motivational effects of previous response outcomes, controls the flow of information between the response planner and the motor system.

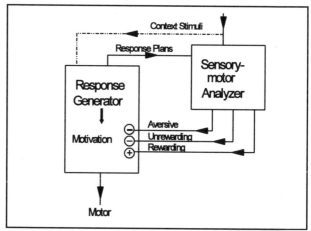

FIG. 2.3.   Outcome dependent response generator.

As will be clear when the anatomy and physiology of these systems are discussed in chapters 8 and 9, the processes of response planning, motivation, and motor output are not located in neat anatomical modules as, for the sake of clarity, they are shown in Fig. 2.3.

Normally, response plans are innately released to the motor system by a facilitatory effect of rewards and blocked by an inhibitory effect of punishment or, more slowly, by the habituating effect of repeated failure to find interesting stimulation. In a particular environment, input from the sensory-motor analyzer to this gating mechanism acquires associations with whatever type of motivational activity is produced by the outcome of a response.

Thus, a spontaneous intention, whose outcome is unpredictable, produces a signal that has no motivational association and passes from planning to execution without interference. A response that is punished, however, is immediately inhibited and replaced by an innate escape response. In such cases the analyzer output (combined effect of the context and the representation of the instrumental response) acquires an association with the response inhibitor, so that subsequent plans to make that response in the same context are aborted.

If, however, the instrumental response is sometimes followed by a reward, the output of the sensory-motor analyzer acquires an association with the process that releases the innate consummatory response elicited by the reward. Subsequent plans to make the instrumental response under similar circumstances reactivate the response release process (which acts nonspecifically on any response being planned), thereby encouraging execution of the plan.

I assume that exploratory responses having outcomes of no innate significance tend to habituate (due to an incrementing inhibitory aftereffect). After habituation has occurred, the output of the analyzer becomes associated with that inhibition. Thus, if the same exploratory response attempts to re-establish itself in the response generator, the analyzer fires neurons associated with response inhibition, discouraging further pursuit of the plan.

If the context changes, the pattern of activity produced in the analyzer, by the new sensory input combined with the response plan, may have no associations, so prediction of the motivational outcome of the response is impossible or unreliable. A response that has habituated in one environment may therefore reappear in a different one, and a previously learned response may no longer receive support.

The mechanism illustrated in Fig. 2.3, is a version of an expectancy learning model (Bolles, 1972; Dickinson & Balleine, 1993; MacCorquodale & Meehl, 1954; Milner, 1960, 1961b; Tolman, 1932). If a rat turns right at the choice point of a Y maze and discovers that it has entered a blind alley, it eventually associates the plan to make that turn with mild response inhibition. If the analyzer had made a mistake and predicted that the response would be rewarded, stronger inhibition would result when the prediction was disconfirmed, eliminating the incorrect response more quickly (see the Discrimination section in chapter 9: p. 115).

A left turn in the maze may lead to the satisfaction of a need, which entails release of a consummatory response. The plan to make a left turn therefore acquires an association with response release or facilitation, increasing the chance that the turn will be executed on subsequent occasions.

To simplify the previous discussion it was assumed that the model generates responses spontaneously, uninfluenced by sensory input. This may be the case in the early stages of learning, when the animal makes random responses or a response acquired previously in a somewhat similar environment. Subsequently, it uses "vicarious trial-and-error" (Tolman, 1932), planning randomly, but failing to execute plans that have no rewarding associations.

Finally, the speed with which a well-practiced response is made suggests that it is no longer chosen randomly. A frequently successful response plan acquires associations from the context (the dotted line in Fig. 2.3), hence it is always the most likely plan to be activated. Response plans continuously compete with each other to become active, so a little help from associated sensory input easily throws the balance in favor of the most frequently and vigorously active response occurring in that context.

Thus, a contextual stimulus present during a response that leads to a reinforcing stimulus, reward or punishment, acquires some of the motivating properties of the reinforcing stimulus itself. The association of the contextual stimulus with the response generator arouses a response plan. Then, in conjunction with the plan it has aroused, the stimulus gives rise to an output of the sensory-motor analyzer that forms an association with the motivational component (or incentive value) of the reinforcing stimulus. In this way a learned response plan acquires control over motivation initially aroused only by the reinforcer.

ATTENTION DURING LEARNED RESPONSES

As mentioned in chapter 1, during learning, associations take place that connect response plans (intentional activity) to engrams of stimuli involved in the performance, not the other way round as postulated in conventional learning theory. A rat that has learned to press a lever to get food not only is put into its feeding mode by the sight of a lever, but also selects sensory input from the lever to guide its approach, suppressing stimuli from, say, the food dispenser, which would seem at first sight to be more closely associated with food.

In the context of the Skinner box, a trained rat first pays attention to the lever. Why is that so? Soon after a rat is first placed in the Skinner box, it investigates everything including the lever and the food tray, an innate reaction to anything moderately novel. At some point during the investigation, sensory input from the lever is selected for delivery to the rat's motor apparatus to guide the investigatory responses. This process is known as selective attention, and it probably involves facilitation of specific sensory input by an output of the current response plan.

If the rat accidentally presses the Skinner-box lever while examining it, causing food to be dispensed, the response, including the attention directed toward sensory input from the lever, acquires an association with food and with the animal's motivation to eat. When this association is strong enough, the engram of the lever receives attentional facilitation whenever the animal is in the mood to eat. Thus, attention to the lever becomes part of the rewarded response plan.

In more general terms, unfamiliar sensory configurations elicit investigation, requiring attention. If nothing interesting transpires, familiarity eventually inhibits the investigatory response, along with the attention that accompanies (or perhaps causes) it. If, however, a reward or punishment occurs during the investigation, the engram of the stimulus acquires associations with the increase in motivation evoked by the reinforcement. Subsequently, any arousal of that motivation activates the engram, which feeds the activation back along a reciprocal attention path to facilitate associated sensory input. If corresponding sensory input is present, it is amplified by the facilitation and further intensifies the engram activation.

SUMMARY

Before attempting to discover how brain activity is related to behavior, it is useful to have in mind a conceptual model that conforms to the behavior to be explained.

Some animals, especially invertebrates, have evolved structures and behaviors that enable them to survive very successfully in suitable environments with a repertoire of mostly innate stereotyped responses. Learning is an evolutionary development that allows animals to augment their instinctive patterns with individually acquired new patterns of behavior.

Approaching and retreating from target objects are almost universal behaviors. They may be modeled by a mechanism that can detect deviations from a direct approach or escape path and use the error information to correct the direction of locomotion.

A complication with the simple model is that when stimuli attempting to guide the animal in different directions are present simultaneously, conflicts arise between error signals, and the guidance system fails. To avoid this difficulty, a mechanism has evolved to ensure that only one of the competing stimuli can control responding at any time. This is the prototype of attention.

Usually, sensory inputs are modulated by signals generated by internal states of the organism (e.g., hunger) before entering the competition to control responding. The winner then inhibits all the runners up. Thus, it alone selects the response plan and ultimately determines which stimuli are allowed access to the motor system to guide the response.

Learning allows animals to approach useful objects more reliably and vigorously, and to avoid exploring dead-ends or repeating bad choices, thus saving time and energy. When no reinforcing stimuli are in evidence, the animal makes random responses, and information about these is combined with contextual sensory input and associated with the motivational outcomes of the responses. Especially important are associations with strong positive or negative affect (which have excitatory or inhibitory effects on centrally organized responses).

Subsequent activity of a response plan in the same context arouses the motivational state aroused by its previous outcome. Thus an initially random response takes on the motivation produced by the reinforcement (if any) that resulted from previous performances. Uneventful explorations are attenuated by habituation, which by its association with the context - response plan combination, reduces the probability of the same response being repeated.

After a number of responses based on internal trial and error, the animal no longer relies on the spontaneous arousal of exploratory response plans. A significant contextual stimulus acquires associations with the response plan that occurs most frequently in that context, ensuring that it is selected first.

The motivation for making a learned response is derived from the reinforcer, but as the motivation has to be effective before the reinforcer is detected by the animal, the reinforcer cannot be the direct target of attention. Attention must be addressed to some other stimulus. Usually this is the stimulus that was being attended to at the time the reinforcer first appeared. Connections between the response plan and this sensory input are therefore strengthened, giving the approach response a "signpost" to the reward as its initial focus of attention.

3 Neural Representation

Every theory of behavior must assume that organisms are capable of responding appropriately to (i.e., recognizing) at least some stimuli. Such behavior implies the existence of brain activities corresponding to external events. The philosophical debate as to whether these representations must be learned, or are innate, has persisted for centuries. After a long period during which most psychologists leaned toward the empiricist view that all recognitions are learned (Locke, 1700/1959), a less radical position is now rapidly gaining favor in the light of evidence from recent neuroanatomical and neuropsychological research (Ishai, Ungerleider, Martin, Maisog, & Haxby, 1997; Kanwisher, McDermott, & Chun, 1997; Kanwisher, Weinrib, Tong, & Nakayama, 1997; Suzuki, Fiorani, & Desimone, 1997; Ungerleider, 1995; Van Essen & Maunsell, 1983) and the impressive advances in genetics and molecular biology reviewed by B. Milner, Squire, and Kandel (1998).

It would seem perverse to maintain that the infant mammal must learn what to do with a nipple, and equally perverse to claim that piloting an airplane is an innate human characteristic, but at the neural level things are not so clear cut. It is quite possible, for example, that visual-system neurons fired by the sight of an airplane do not depend on any previous visual experience with airplanes (though visual experience of some sort is very likely necessary). Clearly, appropriate responses to a novel object must be learned, nevertheless the arousal of a consistent pattern of neural activity by sensory input from the object may be innate.

The more radical empiricists obviously do not subscribe to this view. Hebb (1949), for example, speculated that visual patterns are represented in the nervous system by cell assemblies that take shape gradually from a randomly connected matrix as a result of visual experience. Almost all neural-network modelers assume that the initial state of their networks is random or unrelated to the state of organization needed for effective operation (Hopfield & Tank, 1986; Rumelhart & McClelland, 1986). The neural models must undergo lengthy training to attain a structure capable of performing the desired functions.

It was a tremendous achievement to discover methods of constructing within a few hours or days, simple networks that can emulate behavior that may have taken millions of years to evolve in nature, but it is no more likely that each individual brain has to organize itself by such methods than that cells in the eye destined to become sensitive to light attain that property by individual trial and error.

This does not mean that designing artificial neural networks is of no theoretical value. Apart from providing an efficient way of creating circuits for performing difficult tasks, these networks sometimes show how evolution may have solved a particular problem. Nevertheless, we must beware of assuming that such models tell us anything about what goes on in the developing brain.

PASSIVE AND ACTIVE RECOGNITION

If, as will be argued in this chapter, the neural code representing a stimulus is determined largely by the innate structure of the sensory system, the first thing we would like to know is how the sensory pathways are connected to produce the coded representation. Theoretically, a recognition device may be either passive or active. A passive recognizer acts as a filter that passes only a narrow range of stimulus patterns. It relays selected information, but generates none of its own. An active recognizer, on the other hand, can be active in the absence of the stimulus it recognizes. It may continue to deliver a recognition code for some time after the stimulus has gone, or it may be re-excited at a later time, serving to some extent as a substitute for the stimulus it recognizes. Behaviorists tried unsuccessfully to eradicate the active trace concept from psychology, but the interpretation given to the word "stimulus" constitutes a rather transparent attempt to smuggle it back in.

Simple theories of classical conditioning postulate that passive recognizers, constructed by association, selectively connect conditioned stimuli to responses, but it is extremely doubtful whether such purely passive recognition devices exist in practice. Human beings searching for a misplaced key, or book, usually have a mental image of the desired object. When you call a taxi to go to a restaurant, the taxi and the restaurant are, at the time, figments of your imagination. When the taxi arrives, you recognize it because your brain already exhibits some matching activity.

Even a simple invertebrate that instinctively seeks water when dehydrated, and some sort of shelter or protection when it senses danger, must have neural circuits that respond to different internal states by switching motor control to an appropriate environmental stimulus, a stimulus that may not be present at the time the switching occurs, and therefore must be represented by some corresponding internal activity.

Thus, a primary requirement of a neural representation is that it should be capable of generating activity that matches, in some sense, the sensory input it represents. People, including philosophers and psychologists, are capable of introspection, and hence are well aware that they carry traces of their past that can be reactivated without repeating the experiences that produced them. We call these remnants memories, ideas, images, thoughts, and sometimes more recently adopted names such as engram and cell assembly that refer explicitly to neural representations.

Cell assembly is the name Hebb (1949) gave to his version. *Engram* is a more general name coined by Semon (1921), (Schacter, 1992) and given wider currency by Lashley (1950). Both Hebb and Semon considered the representation to be learned, but I propose to purloin the name "engram" to refer to a neural representation that is selected, rather than constructed, by learning.

DYNAMIC REPRESENTATIONS

One of the first attempts to provide a physiological explanation for active memories was made in 1746 by David Hartley (1959). He suggested that percepts consist of vibrations in the nervous system, and that ideas consist of *vibratiuncles*, weaker vibrations that persist after the perceived object is gone. He also recognized that ideas could be aroused by association with other stimuli or ideas, an important property of active representations not possessed by passive recognizers.

According to Hartley, when two stimuli occur at about the same time their vibrations synchronize so that each can excite vibratiuncles in the other. Thus, in Hartley's theory, the communication between associated ideas is via a broadcast link.

Nearly two centuries later, Lashley (1942), in an effort to explain stimulus equivalence, also proposed that perception involves oscillations. He speculated that interference patterns produced by waves of cortical activity during perception would remain constant despite changes in size and location of the retinal images. Lashley did not, at the time, try to explain the role of the wave patterns in association. That step was taken a few years later by Hebb (1949), a former student of Lashley.

Hebb was aware that the cortex has many recurrent connections and he speculated that during visual perception impulses circulate around complicated loops in this network. Like Hartley, he assumed that the activity persists for some time after the stimulus is removed, a phenomenon he called *reverberation*. Eventually, according to Hebb, the reverberations help to produce synaptic changes that make the network (cell assembly) more likely to fire in the same way later without being triggered by the original stimulus.

EMPIRICIST INFLUENCE

Hebb's (1949) suggestion conforms to the empiricist line that the mind, or brain, of the newborn is a blank page on which experience inscribes representations of surrounding stimuli. Subsequently, if two of the learned representations (cell assemblies) are active at about the same time, they acquire associations with each other in accordance with different learning rules.

Empiricism is a classical theory of knowledge, originating in its more explicit form mainly during the eighteenth century through the writings of Hume (1777/1946) and Locke (1700/1959). It has had an enormous influence on psychological thought ever since psychology became distinct from philosophy. If one is prepared to overlook examples of precocious behavior in the newborn of many animals, it seems a plausible theory, but only as long as no attempt is made to translate it directly into neural terms. Hebb, who made that attempt, was never able to explain why a mass of neurons with random connections that could be strengthened by use did not end up with every neuron associated with every other neuron.

A further puzzle posed by a too literal neural implementation of the empiricist model is that although, over the course of time, one concept may acquire associations with hundreds of others, on any given occasion it normally arouses only one of them. If, as most neural theories of cognition suggest, associations result from the potentiation of synaptic connections between the neurons of different engrams, some mechanism must exist for suppressing most of the connections most of the time. Otherwise, it would be impossible for any engram to fire without bringing about an avalanche of additional engram activity.

Apart from some dyed-in-the-wool behaviorists, psychologists have always known that "set" or intention plays a role, along with sensory input, in determining which of the numerous possible associations influence behavior. Hebb (1949) proposed that set depended on an influence of hypothetical higher-order cell assemblies, but perhaps because of his lack of interest in response mechanisms, he did not delve deeply into the origin of his higher-order assemblies.

THE CELL ASSEMBLY

The reverberatory cell assembly is a seductive idea because it appears to solve, at one stroke, both the problem of the active trace and that of instantaneous memory (which in the days when neural transmission was thought to be electrical was otherwise difficult to explain). The model is still widely accepted, and used in various modified forms, especially by physiologists and computational modelers (Amit, 1995; Braitenberg, 1989; Kaplan, Sonntag, & Chown, 1991; Miller & Wickens, 1991; Mishkin, 1993; Miyashita, 1993; Palm, 1982; Pulvermüller, 1999), but it is fraught with practical difficulties (Milner, 1996).

Immediate memory typically involves many elements: a whole sentence, a telephone number, or the features of a face, which may be changing from moment to moment. In many cases, conceptual elements are replicated. Keeping track of all these different (and sometimes identical) reverberations buzzing around in the same region of the brain, temporarily interrelated yet never coalescing, would be a circuit designer's nightmare.

In view of the unpredictable background activity of the brain, it is unlikely that any activity would remain confined to a fixed path. Each cycle would be different from the last, and repeated presentations of the same stimulus would inevitably fire different groups of neurons.

Furthermore, even if a permanent set of closed loops eventually were to be established, the resulting structure might not do what Hebb intended. Its mode of firing would always be determined more by its internal connections than by the triggering stimulus (Hopfield & Tank, 1986), making it difficult, for example, to discriminate between similar but not identical stimuli, or to perceive and remember unique details, a point raised as long ago as 1959, by Rosenblatt in a conference on self-organizing systems (Milner, 1960, p. 203).

In 1949, when Hebb's theory was published, Eccles (1953) had not yet delivered his pivotal Waynflete Lectures, in which he recanted his earlier vigorous defense of the electrical theory of synaptic transmission and provided convincing evidence for chemical transmission, a much more flexible and versatile mechanism. With chemical transmission, long-term changes in the rate of firing of a neuron are easily accounted for without recourse to feedback reverberation.

AN ALTERNATIVE TO REVERBERATION

Positive feedback is a dangerous tool under the best of circumstances. It would be foolhardy to try to predict how it would behave in a complicated network in which activity-induced changes in connectivity can occur. With increases in the potency of synapses, the reverberations would become more difficult to stop. Attempts to compensate for this by inhibitory damping might prevent reverberation altogether. Considering all the factors, I am convinced that reverberation of impulses around complex learned loops does not play a significant role in the neural representation of stimuli.

A simple alternative to reverberation as a means of maintaining the activity of neural representations was suggested many years ago (Milner, 1957). It involves a temporary sensitization ("priming") of neurons produced by sensory or associational input, so that they can be fired for a time by the non-specific arousal system (Llinas & Ribary, 1993; Moruzzi & Magoun, 1949). The neurons of the trace then continue to fire until they are either inhibited or the priming or arousal input becomes too weak.

Because the neurons of such an engram are activated whether the priming is produced by a recent sensory event or by a previously established association, the circuit retrieves both immediate and long-term memories; an obviously better arrangement than one in which an improbably complicated system is required to interpret neural impulses circulating in unpredictable lattices, while permanently stored material is retrieved by a different method.

An even more promising alternative, to be discussed more fully later, is that the engram of a stimulus consists of neurons driven by input from motor or motivational activity, and involved in selective attention. This is reminiscent of Hebb's idea that attention facilitates cell assemblies, but is more specific.

Invoking motivation-driven attention as the activator of engrams eliminates a number of the difficulties previously mentioned, such as how a stimulus elicits the most relevant concepts from among the large number with which it is associated. It is not the stimulus but the intent, working from the center, that determines which associated engrams are aroused.

STIMULUS EQUIVALENCE IS A DISTRACTION

Like Lashley (1942) and Köhler (Köhler & Wallach, 1944) before him, and many who followed in his footsteps, Hebb (1949) was more interested in explaining stimulus equivalence, a hot topic at the time, than in explaining the role of the cell assembly in learning.

Preoccupation with stimulus equivalence probably stems from the fact that virtually all theories of recognition take an explanation of visual shape perception as their goal. Shape recognition is an accomplishment that is very important for primates, but unfortunately for its investigators, it is achieved by one of our most technically sophisticated sensory systems. The system must make sense of the tenuous relationship between objects to be recognized and the patterns of retinal stimulation to which they give rise. Psychologists studying recognition in the visual system are likely to encounter the phenomenon of stimulus equivalence at an early stage, and it almost always highjacks the investigation.

Stimulus equivalence is a fascinating and important problem discussed at greater length in the next chapter, but it has little to do with the acquisition and association of ideas, processes that already have severe enough problems of their own.

PROBLEMS OF CONCEPT FORMATION

One problem concerns the increased ease of recognition with repeated exposure to a stimulus. How is the recognition threshold for a frequently encountered stimulus lowered without establishing an "attractor" for stimuli that, although similar to the more common one, need to be distinguished from it?

A second problem is the difficulty in understanding why a network consisting of neurons capable of establishing widespread associations with each other does not grow indefinitely as more of the neurons fire at about the same time. The inflated assemblies would then be susceptible to uncontrollable discharge. In the cell-assembly model there is no way of predicting which neurons will participate in which assemblies (and most of them would be expected to participate in more than one). Hence, it is difficult to see how learning synapses between neurons within a cell assembly could differ from those between the neurons in different assemblies.

A major problem for all engram models concerns the density of connections required to ensure that any two engrams may be instantly associated. If you hear someone mention Fats Waller and Hieronymus Bosch in the same sentence, the likely result would be the formation of new associations in your brain, associations that are available for instant use. Such associations hardly could have occurred without pre-existing anatomical contacts between the engrams concerned.

There is no possibility that all the neurons taking part in all the concepts and responses an average person has acquired could have direct connections with each other. The cortex has billions of neurons but few cortical neurons are large enough to accommodate as many as 100,000 synapses. The average for the larger pyramidal cells is probably closer to 30,000. It is true that engrams are made up of many neurons, but if a concept is to be aroused when only a few neurons of its engram are fired by another engram, the neurons constituting the engram must be extensively interconnected. As we saw in the discussion of Hebb's cell assemblies, there are good reasons for rejecting that possibility.

OLFACTION, A SIMPLER SENSE

If dogs (whose ability to discriminate people by smell is almost as astonishing as our ability to discriminate them by sight) could be persuaded to turn their minds to the study of engrams, they would probably not attach as much importance to stimulus equivalence as psychologists do because it plays little part in olfaction. Smells do not have mirror images, nor can they be tilted or (like tunes) transposed to different keys. The same smell always stimulates receptors of the same types. This makes the problem of determining the relation between olfactory input and its neural representation relatively straightforward. The role of the olfactory system in motor control is also much simpler, although less precise, than that of vision or touch.

The olfactory system is not fundamentally different from other sensory systems except in two respects: the virtual absence of any stimulus equivalence mechanism, and the fact that we have no way of simulating olfactory stimulation. We can draw a flower or whistle a birdsong, but the only practical way to communicate information about a smell is to transport the responsible molecules. This removes some of the advantage over other animals that our linguistic and manual skills confer in other sense modalities.

With these reservations, any light that can be cast on the representational process in the olfactory system should be applicable to other modalities, provided input to the system is always taken from the output of any stimulus equivalence circuits the modality may have, not directly from the receptors.

CHEMORECEPTION

Chemoreceptors are a main source of sensory input for single-cell organisms. They have direct links to contractile molecules of the motor system for such purposes as engulfing food particles and escaping from bad environments. Identification of chemical stimuli is performed by the receptor itself, making possible the evolution of appropriate connections with motor molecules, or in more complicated animals that possess nervous systems, with neurons of a motivational system. Hunger, for example, increases sensitivity to food odors and ensures that locomotor mechanisms come under the control of food-sensitive receptors.

Figure 3.1 shows that the mammalian olfactory system resembles other sensory systems in that its input projects to a number of specialized cortical and subcortical areas that return reciprocal connections to the peripheral nuclei. Connections between the olfactory bulb and the olfactory tubercle probably serve innate functions, whereas links to the periamygdaloid and entorhinal cortex are probably related to the association of odors with each other and with other stimuli. The connections to the amygdala appear to serve both innate and learned functions.

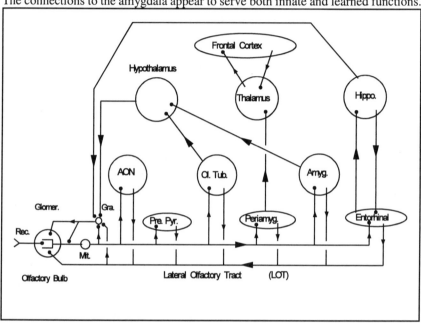

FIG. 3.1.   Olfactory system.
Amyg.- amygdala; AON - Anterior olfactory nucleus; Glomer.- glomerulus; Gra.- granule cell; Hippo.- hippocampus; Mit.- mitral cell; Ol. Tub.- olfactory tubercle; Periamyg.- periamygdaloid cortex; Pre. Pyr.- pre-pyriform cortex; Rec.- receptor.

The afferent paths comprise the axons of mitral and tufted cells from the olfactory bulb that course through the lateral olfactory tract (LOT). The LOT also carries reciprocal connections from the cortical and subcortical projection areas back to the olfactory bulb. In the olfactory bulb, large numbers of receptors converge on a few thousand small clusters of mitral and tufted-cell dendrites in structures known as glomeruli. The glomeruli are interconnected via periglomerular neurons and reciprocal dendro-dendritic synapses of granule cells. Feedback from olfactory nuclei and the cortex reaches all the neurons of the bulb via the LOT (Shepherd, 1987).

It seems likely that in the mammalian olfactory system there are at least several hundred different receptor proteins, some binding only a few closely related odor molecules, others being sensitive to a broader spectrum of odors. Evidence indicates that each receptor cell expresses only one type of odor-binding protein, and that cells whose axons converge on a given glomerulus all express the same protein

(Buck, 1996; Hildebrand & Shepherd, 1997).

Odors are mapped by the glomeruli of the olfactory bulb in much the same way as visual stimuli are mapped by the ganglion cells of the retina. Odors with related molecular structure produce overlapping fields, just as colors of similar wavelength, or adjacent spots of light, produce overlapping fields in the visual system.

Receptors having the same receptor protein converge on a glomerulus with little, if any, lateral spread. Thus, each of the several thousand glomeruli receives sensory input corresponding to the sensitivity profile of only one of the receptor proteins. After this point in the path, due to the action of periglomerular cells that connect neighboring glomeruli, as well as feedback from granule cells and recurrent LOT fibers, it is impossible to predict the exact firing pattern of cells contributing to the afferent LOT.

INNATE RECOGNITION

Much of the LOT feedback is inhibitory, presumably preventing weakly stimulated glomeruli from contributing to the afferent stream. Li (1994) has suggested that it also plays a role in adaptation to smells. Furthermore, excitatory feedback from central structures probably emphasizes the signals produced by any odor related to current motivation. Innate reciprocal paths (e.g., from the hypothalamus) might increase the sensitivity of glomeruli that respond to sexual attractants, odors of food, poisons, or enemies, depending on the prevailing motivational state.

These recurrent connections can be regarded as innate representations of stimuli because, when active, they change the way the animal responds to a specific stimulus. If the animal, under the influence of a hormone or other change in body chemistry, is motivated to seek some reinforcer such as food or a sexual partner, part of the activity aroused in the motivation system contains a description of olfactory stimulation that may be pertinent to the behavior.

This description, delivered to the olfactory pathway, ensures that if there is a matching sensory input, it is selected and given access to locomotor controls (possibly via the olfactory tubercle, which has characteristics similar to those of other basal ganglia; see chapter 8). Thus the smell of food, for example, determines where the animal goes.

It is important to understand that innate recognition is a function of the motivation system, not of the sensory path. The sensory path must be ready to transmit any information that arrives. From this input the motivation system selects whatever is needed for the current task and ensures that it reaches the motor system. This is possible due to connections made by the motivation neurons during development. As a result of natural selection the response system can recognize olfactory-path neurons likely to be carrying information required for a task and synapse with them to gain control over their sensitivity.

PERCEPTUAL LEARNING

Psychologists are less interested in innate mechanisms than in knowing how innately significant stimuli acquire *new* associations, and how stimuli with no innate connections acquire associations that make them useful.

Like monochromatic light, a monomolecular olfactory stimulus excites more than one type of receptor, some more strongly than others. Pure amyl acetate, for example, binds with varying degrees of effectiveness to several receptor proteins to produce a characteristic pattern of glomerular stimulation and LOT firing (Kauer, 1991). Just as most pigments reflect many different wavelengths of light, most smells result from combinations of different odorant molecules, which produce more complex patterns of LOT activity.

There are between 100 and 1,000 different types of olfactory receptor in mammals, each type projecting to a different group of glomeruli. In most mammals, each glomerulus contributes 50 to 100 axons to the LOT. It would seem therefore that activity corresponding to the odor profile of each receptor is delivered to the olfactory areas by hundreds of parallel paths, a good proportion of which probably find their way to the cortex.

The potential number of different odor patterns, even if each fiber had only two states, on and off, would be about 2^n, where n is the number of different receptor types. With an n of 200, the number of potential patterns would be about 10^{50} times the number of neurons in the human brain. Clearly, even single synapses could represent only a minuscule fraction of the total number of possible different smells.

A probable mechanism is that some cortical neurons (primary sensory neurons) receive excitatory and inhibitory inputs from assorted branches of LOT fibers. These neurons may be regarded as templates. If an odor produces a pattern of LOT firing that includes most of the excitatory afferents to a cortical neuron and none or only a few of its inhibitory afferents, the neuron will be strongly excited by that odor. In the olfactory system, the step from receptor to neural representation could be short and simple!

The next important question is: How does the firing of a particular pattern of olfactory cortex neurons acquire meaning. As already mentioned, some neurons are innately connected to initiate vital response plans. In many cases, however, with repeated stimulation, the connections weaken for a time. The receptors continue to respond to the odor, so it is assumed that the adaptation occurs in the sensory path (Li, 1994). The simplest explanation is that synapses in the path undergo long-term depression (LTD), a primitive form of learning.

A more interesting possibility is that the sensory path is inhibited by neurons that continue to fire for a time after they have responded to a stimulus, thus constituting an active trace. Active traces are discussed more fully later in this chapter. As discussed earlier (p. 25), it is my belief that they consists of neurons whose connections to a continuously active source of facilitatory pulses (a clock) are turned on for a short time by a stimulus input. It is likely that all sensory inputs establish active traces of a similar nature, as temporary stores for incoming signals.

Cortical neurons fired by a smell become engrams of that smell when they acquire reciprocal synaptic connections with neurons that are active in the emotion, motivation, and response-generating complex during the time the smell is present. This makes the cortical neurons equivalent to neurons that have innate connections for indicating the presence of some needed or alarming stimulus. The firing of some olfactory neurons may be associated, for example, with apprehension and a plan to pronounce the word "fire," others with satisfaction and a plan to say "coffee." A dog may be taught to bark when it smells dynamite.

Not all smells acquire associations with a need or response plan, but if the smell is to be recognized later, the cortical neurons they fire must establish associations with something. The ability to recall events in relation to other events and to the passage of time, often called episodic memory, is discussed in chapter 6.

SEGMENTATION OF ODORS

If the pattern of LOT firing changes for any reason, different cortical neurons will be maximally stimulated. Adding the smell of chocolate to that of strawberries, for example, might be expected to fire neurons not fired by either of the components, producing a new smell in which possibly neither odor would be recognizable.

In some cases this happens. Mixing ingredients to create new fragrances is an art. However, many smells retain their distinctiveness when mixed. For example, it is not difficult to detect that someone has been eating garlic and drinking alcohol because the olfactory system does not always merge incoming odors completely. The need for segmentation is not confined to olfaction. Vision would be almost useless if we had no way of distinguishing objects from their background and saw each combination of shapes and colors as a new stimulus.

Li (1994) proposed that segmentation in the olfactory system results from adaptation, but this would depend on a new smell being added to one that had been present for some time. If two familiar stimuli were presented simultaneously, adaptation could not be a factor. Nevertheless, Li's suggestion that segmentation involves feedback is very plausible. Odors of no consequence usually acquire inhibitory associations with the motivational system and stop being attended to. Thus they interfere less with other odors present at the time. A mixture of novel odors does not differ from any other novel olfactory stimulus in that it fires a unique pattern of sensory neurons which may be associated with a name or some other response plan.

Theory suggests that cortical neurons frequently fired by a significant stimulus are activated more easily by weak or partial stimulation. The activity could then inhibit conflicting inputs via feedback to earlier sensory levels. This suggests that odors can be segmented only if they have an innate meaning, or a meaning acquired by frequent association with some response or motivational state. An odor could acquire such a meaning only by occurring alone or at a much stronger intensity than background odors before it occurred in a mixture.

When two familiar odors are mixed, neither produces as strong an effect on its own central associations as it does when alone, but each may nevertheless elicit its usual meaning and receive facilitation, at least intermittently. Both smells can usually be distinguished, but if they are presented together frequently, the pattern of neurons fired by the mixture eventually acquires its own associations and thus becomes a distinct engram.

Segmentation is of prime importance in all sense modalities. In the visual system, as described later, theoretical considerations (Milner, 1974; von der Malsburg, 1994) and measurements of the activity of single cortical units (Gray, König, Engel, & Singer, 1989) support the idea that figure - ground segregation depends, at least partly, on synchronous firing of cortical neurons representing the figure. Oscillatory potentials are seen in the olfactory bulb during sensory stimulation, but their relation to segmentation of odors has not been demonstrated with certainty.

MECHANISMS OF CORTICAL ASSOCIATION

In most of the cortex, neurons tend to be interconnected to form vertical columns. These columns act as super-neurons, with large input and output capacities (Tanaka, 1992). In the present model of the engram cortex it is assumed that columns responding to the same or similar stimuli are distributed randomly throughout the area. Such an anatomical configuration would explain why small cortical lesions rarely eliminate a specific item of behavior, but cause a general deterioration that depends on the extent of the lesion (*mass action*).

As described earlier, receptors are linked to cortical neurons during development, probably according to some genetically determined design, so that even before the animal has taken its first breath, olfactory stimuli are represented by specific combinations of afferent fiber terminals on cortical neurons. The representation may be enhanced in various ways by learning, but it is functional at birth. Until some learning has occurred, however, activity of the representational neurons is meaningless. It is possible that some cortical neurons have innate connections with neurons of the motivation systems, but most innate connections are probably subcortical.

The firing of primary sensory neurons provides the raw data that animals learn to use for many purposes. Dogs can use the information to learn olfactory skills such as detecting explosives or drugs. A connoisseur of wine can learn to assess the quality of a Moselle or a Burgundy. How is this done? If an intelligent hound is given a morsel of a favorite food when it finds and investigates a stick of dynamite, it soon catches on to the game and approaches the source whenever the smell is detected. The usual explanation for the dog's behavior is that it acquires an engram representing the smell of the explosive and associates it with an engram of the reward. It is the idea of the reward that motivates the dog to keep searching.

The wine connoisseur also plays a game in which she derives pleasure from the correct recognition of a sample and is dismayed by errors. Success requires that attention be directed to components of the wine bouquet she has associated with other properties of the wine, such as its age and provenance.

New percepts often become intelligible as they resolve themselves into combinations of established percepts, evidence that representations, far from being assimilated into concurrent cortical activity, retain their distinctiveness. It is certain that a name can help people to see an indistinct stimulus by activating its engram, thereby enlisting attentional facilitation. Instructing a person to look for an arch-shaped structure in a fuzzy picture speeds up the perception. Similarly, hearing the word cherry may draw attention to one component of a complex taste.

By the expression "draw attention to" we probably mean facilitation of the neurons that are normally excited by the stimulus in question. This can be done only if a word such as "cherry" directly or indirectly facilitates neurons stimulated by the appearance and taste of cherries. According to the proposed model, engrams are the initial targets of attention, and attention arises from an intention to perform a response that satisfies some urge or need. A stimulus that arouses an intention indirectly facilitates the engrams of things associated with that intention.

THE ACTIVE CORTICAL TRACE

Little, if anything, is known about the detailed structure of engrams, but a lot is known about what they accomplish. Figure 3.2 exemplifies a type of hypothetical circuit intended to illustrate the problems that confront actual perceptual systems. Diagrams of this sort may be helpful in explaining how a neural mechanism works, but they also can be misleading. Because a single "neuron" of the figure represents many thousands of real neurons, the diagrams usually fail to convey the stochastic nature of the information processing performed by most brain circuits.

Another reason why the details of such circuits need not be taken too seriously is that there are many different ways of achieving a particular outcome. However, the tasks the circuits are designed to perform *should* be taken seriously. Taking note of the requirements of a particular performance may help us to discover how it is achieved by our nervous systems.

The circuit of Fig. 3.2 is based on the olfactory system. In that system, as explained earlier, the relation between receptor activity and the neural representation of a stimulus is simpler than in other sense modalities. If the signals from the receptors stimulated by a smell eventually converge on a cortical neuron, activity of that neuron contributes to the representation of the smell. The connections by which this comes about are genetically determined. Output of the odor-detecting neurons is used to regulate behavior, so it must provide a stable representation of the stimulus.

In most sense modalities a stimulus leaves a temporary trace that, amongst

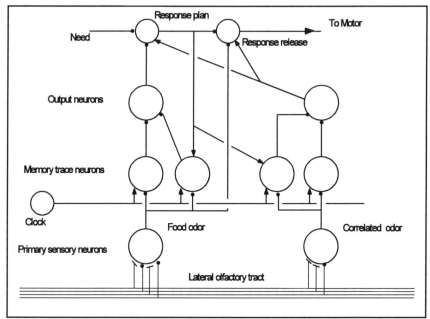

FIG. 3.2.   Olfactory engram circuits.

other things, enables animals to associate the stimulus with other neural events that follow shortly afterwards. Without such a trace we would have no sense of time. We would be unable to interpret, or even detect, changes of a stimulus.

This neural trace is the first level of memory. It is unaffected by lesions of the hippocampal area that produce severe deficits of longer term storage (see chapter 6), so presumably it involves an early stage of the sensory path. In Fig. 3.2 sensory signals from a single primary odor neuron feed directly onto two active-trace neurons. The outputs of the two neurons then converge onto a single output neuron.

The point of having duplicate neurons in parallel at the active trace stage of the circuit is to suggest a means whereby the capacity for associative inputs (mainly from response plans) may be increased. It is possible that many of the interneurons in cortical columns serve this function (Tanaka, 1992). Afferents from all response plans must be accommodated, even though the majority of the paths may never be used.

The trace neurons also receive input from a source of non-specific activation labeled "clock" in Fig. 3.2 by analogy with similar sources of repetitive drive pulses in electronic equipment. The synapses from the clock are ineffective until the trace neuron fires. They are then potentiated for a time, enabling the clock input to keep the neuron firing repeatedly until the potentiation decays or the neuron is inhibited.

Because they continue to fire after their sensory input has disappeared, trace neurons can become part of an active engram of the stimulus. In Fig. 3.2 the output neurons of the columns are shown as having learning synapses with neurons in the response planning system. They are potentiated when a response plan and trace neurons are active at the same time.

ASSOCIATIVE LEARNING

Suppose the odor detected by the circuit under discussion is that of a person who brings the animal its meal. The simplified circuitry for eating is represented in Fig. 3.2 by two "neurons," a response-planning neuron and a response-release neuron. These circuits, which appear to be located in the basal ganglia and prefrontal cortex (Fuster, 1997), are discussed more fully in chapters 8 and 9.

The chemical state of the body determines the threshold, or activation level, of the plan to eat. The plan has innate connections to engrams of food stimuli, sensitizing the hungry animal to the odors of some foods. Preliminaries to eating such as salivation and gastric secretion can be executed in the absence of stimuli from food, especially if a stimulus conditioned to food is present, but plans to approach and consume food obviously cannot be formulated until the location of the food is known.

When food has been located, the movements needed to approach it can be computed by the response planner (Wise, Boussaoud, Johnson, & Caminiti, 1997). Simultaneously, the response-release mechanism is activated by sensory input from the food. The engram for the conditioned stimulus (in this case the smell of the person bringing the meal) continues to be active while the neurons representing the plan to eat are firing, allowing associations to be established in both directions between the two groups of neurons. The "person" engram also acquires an association with the response-release mechanism when the latter is innately activated by the food.

The release mechanism is common to all response plans. It releases whichever planned response is dominant at the time it is activated. As stated previously, no plan to approach and eat food can be organized in the absence of food, but when the response-release system is activated by its association with the food-delivery person, responses such as salivation and other autonomic preparations for eating are released. These preparations are frequently accompanied by vocalization, approach to the person, and an increase in random or stereotyped activity. The innate facilitation of the food engram is also intensified by the plan to eat, increasing the animal's sensitivity to stimuli from food when it is present. Activation of the food engram by the plan to eat may correspond to thinking about food, and in human beings might involve requesting food.

On later occasions, when the animal becomes hungry again and the motivation system is dominated by plans to eat, the association between the response plan and the engram of the person who brings food is reactivated. The animal is thus sensitized to the approach of its caretaker, much as it is sensitized to stimuli from food. It is to be hoped, however, especially if the animal is large, that the response of eating still requires sensory input specifically from the food.

It should be noticed that according to this account ideas are associated with each other via the response system. Stimuli from a person elicit plans to eat. They in turn facilitate engrams representing food. Similarly, other stimuli that establish an intention to eat may lead to the facilitation of neurons that represent the smell of the food provider. In people, a smell of food may evoke plans to pronounce its name, arousing engrams for the sound of the name, and so on.

It is difficult to think of any simple, plausible alternative to the idea that associations usually involve the mediation of response plans. Perhaps frequently co-activated engrams sometimes acquire direct facilitatory links with each other, though the links must never become strong enough to cause the engrams to merge. However, to make it possible for all concepts to acquire direct associations with all other concepts without any delay, every neuron in every engram would need potential learning synapses with every other engram neuron. That would produce a chaotic and anatomically impossible mass of connections.

Another example of association via responses is that between screws and screwdrivers. Although strongly associated by most people, the objects are never confused. If a door handle is loose, requiring its screw to be tightened, the intention to perform that task is associated with the concept of a screwdriver and attention is directed to finding one. The association between the screw and the screwdriver is via the task of tightening the screw. An intention to manufacture a screw, would instead have elicited an association with a lathe or a die.

There are, of course, situations in which associations do not involve responses or motivation. For example, the smell of cigar smoke might be associated with a passer by. This event might have been associated with a place and a time, but not with a response. As discussed in chapter 6, such episodic associations may be via a continuous flow of neural activity (unrelated to any specific response) to which sequences of events automatically become associated as they occur, thereby becoming linked to each other.

Even if associations between concepts normally take place via the response system, the process must still require many potential connections. Every engram must be connected in such a way that it can instantly acquire an association from every response plan. Nevertheless, this should be less expensive in connections than the alternative of having all engrams directly accessible to each other, because whereas for all practical purposes there is no limit to the number of different concepts that can be acquired, most response plans consist of different sequences of a relatively few basic movements. Sequential information can be conveyed much more economically than parallel information. Speech, for example, can carry very complicated information via a single pair of wires.

There are about 500 different muscles in the human body. All our masterpieces and monstrosities have been produced by various combinations, intensities, and sequences of activation of only a few hundred different effectors. An ability to interpret sequential codes may well be crucial for complex thought processes. This subject is discussed further in chapter 5, which deals with the learning of words.

STIMULUS MATCHING

One of the most common perceptual tasks is the comparison of current sensory input with a recently experienced sample. To do this, the pattern of sensory activity occurring during the sample must be stored by immediate memory neurons until the stimulus with which it is to be compared is presented.

Investigators (Chelazzi, Miller, Duncan, & Desimone, 1993; Fuster, Bauer, & Jervey, 1985; Miyashita, 1993) have found that after an animal has learned to obtain a reward by choosing an object similar to one it was shown a short time earlier, some neurons activated by the sample object continue to fire during the interval before the choice objects are presented. A common assumption is that these neurons are part of a reverberating cell assembly, but, of course, the assumption made here is that they are active trace neurons like those shown in Fig. 3.2.

The trace neurons must continue to fire until their activity has been compared with input from the subsequently presented choice objects. When the trace neurons are fired by the sample, their synapses from a drive input, such as the non-specific activating system, are potentiated and, as previously described, their activity is maintained for a time by that input. As long as they are fired in this way no further sensory input must be allowed to reach them.

Comparison of the persisting activity of the storage neurons with the activity of neurons representing the current stimulus might be accomplished by comparator neurons fired by the trace neurons and inhibited by matching current input. Then, if any comparator neurons fire, the viewed object must be different from the sample.

Fuster et al. (1985) discovered that during the delay time between the presentation of a visual sample (color) and the presentation of a choice of stimuli for matching, neurons in both the prefrontal (response plan) cortex and the inferotemporal (object recognition) cortex continue to fire. Blocking the activity of the prefrontal cells by cooling usually reduced the activity of the inferotemporal cortex neurons during the delay. Cooling the inferotemporal cortex tended to increase the activity of prefrontal neurons.

This finding is consistent with the hypothesis that the source of continuing input to the response plan neurons during the delay is motivation to receive a reward, and that the activity of the response-plan neuron is important for the continued firing of the neurons corresponding to the trace of the sample stimulus. The result does not support the idea that the frontal and temporal neurons are joint participants in a reverberating loop. If that were the case, the prediction would be for each area to be affected in the same way when the other is cooled.

SUMMARY

How we associate ideas may be the oldest problem in psychology. As long as ideas were thought to exist only in a remote mental sphere, beyond the scope of worldly science, most psychologists were content merely to specify the conditions under which associations take place. Classical behaviorists formalized this attitude by decreeing certain processes mental, and therefore off limits.

Physiological psychologists have no such escape hatch. If thoughts are based on neural activity, then it should be possible to discover what happens to the neurons when one idea leads to another. At present, a widely accepted hypothesis is that stimuli are represented by cell assemblies (Amit, 1995; Goltsev, 1996; Miller & Wickens, 1991), structures postulated by Hebb (1949, 1980) to be produced by associations between neurons that fire together during perception.

An appealing feature of the cell assembly is that it can be active in the absence of the stimulus it represents and aroused by association with other cell assemblies. Unfortunately, the mechanisms proposed for achieving these features are difficult to reconcile with present anatomical and neurophysiological knowledge.

Moreover, Hebb (1949) developed his model almost entirely with respect to the visual system. Thus a disproportionate effort was devoted to an attempt to solve the problem of stimulus equivalence, a problem that is peripheral to the basic problems of stimulus representation and association.

There are fewer distractions in the olfactory system, where the main stimulus variables are molecular structure and concentration. Stimulus equivalence is not an issue here because a given substance always stimulates the same receptors. This is not true of the visual system, in which an object almost never stimulates the same pattern of retinal receptors on repeated presentation.

The connections between olfactory receptors and cortical neurons laid down during development determine the response of each neuron to a particular odor. Thus, the pattern of neural activity that corresponds to an odor is already established before birth. Even the meaning of some of the neural activity, the activity induced by pheromones or food, for example, is innately determined.

In many animals, however, the meaning of most engram activity is learned. The plan of a response whose occurrence is correlated with the perception of a stimulus acquires associations with trace neurons activated by the stimulus. Thus the plan may eventually be evoked by the stimulus, or, equally significant for behavior, planning to execute the response evokes the trace of the stimulus.

Hebb's (1949) empiricist proposal that stimuli are represented by opportunistic connections between cortical neurons that form reverberating loops is inconsistent with what is now known about the fixed cortical localization of visual categories, such as scenes and faces. It is also considered unlikely, on neurophysiological grounds, that the observed active trace neurons continue to fire as a result of feedback reverberation. A more plausible explanation for their activity, once it has been initiated by a stimulus, is that it is maintained by input from a source of clock pulses, possibly the "chattering" cells of Gray and McCormick (1996), or by input from response-plan neurons activated by motivational input. Other storage neurons, possibly enabled by an instruction from the motor system, allow the engram of a sample stimulus to be retained until it can be compared with stimuli presented later.

The feature of engrams that is fundamentally important for behavior is their ability to be activated by association as well as by sensory input. The human ability to associate ideas has been known for thousands of years. Recently, partly as a consequence of cell-assembly theory, this process has been attributed to direct associations between engrams, but it is difficult to imagine how every engram can be in constant contact with every other engram, a necessity if our ability to form instantaneous arbitrary associations is to be explained. The parts of the puzzle may be summarized as follows:

- Most of our concepts cannot be represented by genetically determined neural processes. Objects and abstractions of recent origin cannot yet have influenced our genetic makeup and their concepts must therefore be learned.
- It is difficult to understand how a network of neurons capable of establishing widespread associations with each other can be prevented from growing indefinitely as a result of frequent co-stimulation. The expanding networks would then be liable to uncontrollable discharge.
- Because empiricist theories offer no way of predicting which neurons in such networks will be recruited into which engrams (and almost certainly most will belong to more than one), it would be impossible to have learning synapses linking neurons in different engrams while none link the neurons within an engram.

Early behaviorists, who believed that ideas had no place in a scientific theory, thought that stimuli could become associated only with responses. They may have been half right, but responses can also become associated with stimuli. Selective attention appears to entail the establishment of associations between intentions and the engrams of stimuli that have been found useful in the execution of the intended actions. Thus, it may not be too far-fetched to suggest that when a stimulus evokes a response plan, the plan evokes other related engrams. Indirect association of engrams, via response plans or some related neural activity, would seem less likely to produce a neural log jam than would a process involving direct association. Recordings of neuron activity during delayed matching in animals supports the hypothesis that motivated response plans are responsible for maintaining the activity of those neurons storing sensory information during the waiting period.

4 Stimulus Equivalence and Attention

A smell always stimulates the same receptors except for minor differences in left - right intensity, immediately revealing the familiarity and desirability (or otherwise) of its source. Smells can be detected at a distance, which makes them useful for guiding locomotion. The olfactory sense is less useful for supervising manipulatory responses. For that, animals without vision use mainly tactual receptors of the face and mouth and, in some cases, paws.

Vision supplements both of these more primitive senses. The recognition and evaluative functions of smell are augmented by a ventral visual path that borders the olfactory system in the ventral temporal lobe. A dorsal visual pathway extending into the parietal lobe contributes to manipulatory control (Goodale, Milner, Jakobson & Carey, 1991; Goodale & Milner, 1992; Ungerleider & Mishkin, 1982; Van Essen & Maunsell, 1983).

Stimulus equivalence is important for the ventral recognition process. It ensures that all the different patterns of retinal stimulation produced by a certain category of objects fire at least some common neurons at a central level of the visual pathway. Recognition is not necessary in the dorsal pathway, but the signal there is processed to take account of head and eye position. Nevertheless, only visual input produced by the object of interest is allowed to influence the motor system via this route.

The visual signal thus delivers instant and accurate information about the identity and whereabouts of a stimulus. The catch is that there are no neurons in the system that do both. Yet for an animal to approach a food dish, for example, its motor system must be guided almost exclusively by directional information from neurons fired specifically by the dish. How this is achieved has been a long-standing puzzle.

It is important to understand that the stimulus equivalence problem concerns mainly shape recognition. When color, for example, is an adequate clue to the identity of an object, stimulus equivalence is not so important. Some neurons selective for color have small fields, so averaging the output from a cluster of such neurons makes it possible to pinpoint the direction of a colored object relative to the direction of gaze. The position of the object in relation to the body can then be computed by circuits in the parietal cortex (Maunsell, 1995; Wise et al., 1997).

For a similar reason, stimuli that move relative to neighboring visual stimuli, are also easy to localize. Nevertheless, the fact remains that mammals, and especially primates, visually identify most objects by their shape which, except for very simple shapes, is represented by neurons with extensive fields that provide almost no localizing information.

EARLY THEORIES

That different receptors are excited from moment to moment by an unchanging visual scene as a result of head and eye movements did not upset classical behaviorists as much as it should have. They merely moved what they misnamed the stimulus (S) inboard a notch or two and said it was the job of perceptual psychologists, not learning theorists, to discover how it was related to receptor activity.

Gestalt psychologists took the matter more seriously. They thought stimulus equivalence could be accounted for by an innate property of visual systems that they considered analogous to a field effect in physics. Köhler believed that the projection of an input onto the visual cortex produced an electrical field that did not change significantly on displacement of the visual image (Köhler & Wallach, 1944). How the field was supposed to influence behavior was never made clear. Gestalt psychologists appear to have believed that once an isomorphic representation of the stimulus was delivered to the mind, the mind would look after it from there on.

Lashley (1942) also thought stimulus equivalence was an innate property of the visual cortex. He asked himself:

> By what possible mechanisms might a pattern of stimulation, exciting one restricted group of nerve cells, set up a reproduction of itself, reduplicated throughout the whole cerebral area into which those nerve cells discharge? (Lashley, 1942, p. 312)

He went on to speculate that the projection of visual input onto the cortex excited oscillations in the "loops of various lengths and complexity" (Lashley, 1942, p .313) discovered by Lorente de Nó (1938). Lashley (1942) suggested that these oscillations spread across the cortex, interacting with each other to establish reduplicated interference patterns that he claimed would be unaffected by changes in the position of the stimulus. Neither Lashley's theory, nor Köhler's, withstood experimental analysis.

Hebb (1949), as previously mentioned, rejected the nativist view and suggested that different inputs generated by the same object become associated with the same cell assembly (also concocted from the fruit of Lorente de Nó's research). This theory has proved difficult to test experimentally, but some criticisms of his empiricist solution were presented in chapter 3.

Stemming from Hebb's hypothesis, a number of learning networks have been modeled by computer to simulate various aspects of perception, including stimulus equivalence. Rosenblatt (1962) understood, like Lashley, that some mechanism for replication was necessary, and hidden among the mathematics of his book on perceptron theory is the concept of convergence as a means of generalizing (p. 327).

In any case, creating effective connections in a simulated neural network

(Rumelhart & McClelland, 1986) requires that the model undergo an exorbitant amount of training, which reinforces the impression that cell assemblies cannot be learned quickly or reliably enough to explain the visual capabilities of newborn infants (Kaye & Bower, 1994; Meltzoff & Moore, 1989; Walton, Bower, & Bower, 1992; Walton & Bower, 1993). No doubt over many generations a mechanism for stimulus equivalence has evolved by Darwinian trial and error, but it seems unreasonable to suppose that every individual must learn it from scratch. After all, it is hardly conceivable that evolution, a process that achieved such engineering marvels as the eye and the ear, would abandon the outputs of these organs to fend for themselves in a wilderness of randomly tangled neurons.

THE PROBLEM OF OBJECT LOCATION

For an individual to select an object for manipulation, or even just fixation, neurons that carry information about the precise location of the object relative to the body must be available. The problem is that there are no neurons in the retina or in the primary visual cortex that represent only a particular object (a ball for example, or the letter A). At one moment the field of a neuron in the primary visual cortex may be occupied by part of the image of a ball, and a moment later, after either the ball or the eye has moved, by part of the image of a tree. Attending to a ball cannot involve the direct facilitation of "ball" neurons in the primary visual cortex because no ball-specific neurons exist there.

Nevertheless, because we can recognize a ball when we see it, we know that somewhere in the visual system are neurons that fire when a ball (or something resembling a ball) is within their visual fields. Sensitizing those neurons by attention certainly would alert us to the presence of a ball, but the ball might be anywhere in the visual field because the neurons respond to anything recognizable as a ball, wherever it is (Desimone, Albright, Gross, & Bruce, 1984; Perrett et al., 1991; Perrett, Rolls, & Caan, 1982). Representing all objects at every different size, orientation, and location with a separate group of neurons for each, would require an impossibly large brain.

Circuits responsible for stimulus equivalence lie between the retinotopic level of the visual system, where the stimulus can be located but not identified, and the recognition level, where the neurons that identify the stimulus provide little serviceable positional information. Apparently the equivalence circuits must carry information in both directions so that visual input can be recognized at the central level and the facilitatory power of attention can influence retinotopic neurons, whose activity provides the positional information needed by the motor system to manipulate the object.

This bidirectional transmission is another reason for doubting that the neural code for a stimulus is learned, as empiricist theories propose. If that were the case, then the recurrent attention paths would have to be learned as well, further complicating an already incomprehensible process.

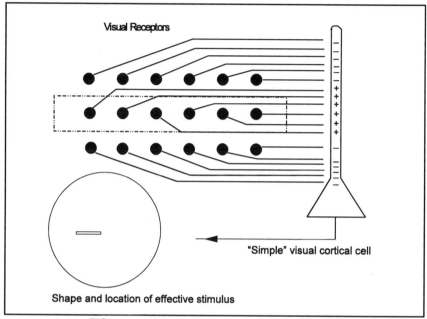

FIG. 4.1.   Connections of "simple" visual cells.

INNATE RECOGNITION OF LINES

To escape the problems resulting from the fact that any receptor may participate in the perception of any stimulus, stimulus equivalence circuits must be based on an initial stage of innate pattern recognition. Hubel and Wiesel (1959), while recording from neurons in the cat's primary visual cortex, made the well-known discovery that neurons respond maximally to lines at specific positions in the visual field and oriented in a particular direction.

To explain these properties of the neurons, it was proposed that they receive excitatory input (via the thalamus) from a row of receptors, along with inhibitory input from receptors bordering that row. Thus, a strip of light confined to the receptors that have excitatory connections to a neuron causes the neuron to fire. If the strip is made wider, however, so that it encroaches on the bordering rows of receptors with inhibitory connections to the cell, firing slows, and when the strip of light is wide enough, stops (Fig. 4.1). Hubel and Wiesel, 1959) called these neurons "simple" cells to distinguish them from "complex" cells (Fig. 4.2), which they also found in the visual cortex. Complex cells respond to lines having a particular orientation wherever they are located within a large region of the visual field.

GENERALIZATION BY CONVERGENCE

The investigators postulated that complex cells are fired by converging input from many simple line cells, each responding to a line in a different part of the visual field. As the stimulus line moves from place to place in the field, it fires different simple cells, each of which in turn takes over the task of firing the complex cell on which they all converge. This hypothesis is now thought to be an oversimplification (Hoffmann & Stone, 1971). Complex cells may combine the functions of both cell types, but the principle is probably correct.

The outputs of line cells of differing orientation may be combined to fire cells

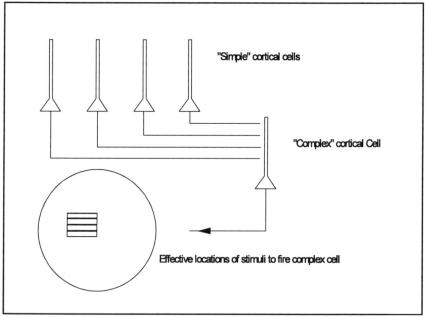

FIG. 4.2. Connections between "simple" and "complex" cells in the visual cortex.

representing more complex figures. If a neuron fires as a result of converging input from simple cells that represent vertical and horizontal lines, for example, it will represent a right angle. Right angles then may be generalized over the field by connecting the outputs of many right-angle detectors to an output cell that may be fired by a right angle in any part of the field.

Firing of other neurons may require summation of the outputs of neurons fired by two or three samples of a line or other figure element, providing an indication of the number of those elements in a figure. In this way, by recognizing, generalizing, and counting a small selection of simple figure elements, patterns of activated neurons can represent complex figures, wherever and of whatever size and orientation they appear on the retina (Biederman, 1987; Hummel & Biederman, 1992; Milner, 1974; Rosenblatt, 1962).

Some years ago, based on this principle, I wrote a computer program for recognizing simple figures. One version of the program not only recognizes whole figures, it also responds to questions about the presence of other figures (whose names it has previously learned) embedded in the figure.[1]

In the same way that a smell is represented by many neurons scattered throughout the olfactory cortex, a single visual stimulus is represented by very many neurons in the inferotemporal cortex, as is revealed by microelectrode recording and imaging studies (Desimone et al., 1984; Gross, Bender, & Rocha-Miranda, 1969; Ishai et al., 1997; Kanwisher, McDermott et al., 1997).

In general, no neuron represents only a single figure. Each of the neurons comprising the engram of a house, for example, may be fired by a range of other retinal images. It is the combination of fired neurons that is unique to a particular image, and, according to the hypothesis adopted in this book, the group acquires a specific meaning by becoming associated with a particular pattern of motivational or intentional activity.

Thus, there is no such thing as a grandmother cell (Barlow, 1972), only a lot of "could be grandma" cells, along with an absence of "could not be grandma" cells. "Grandmother" is the arousal of an emotion and probably a variety of responses, including verbal responses, by the firing of a collection of high-order sensory neurons. Individually, the neurons of the group may fire in response to a host of different stimuli, but when enough of them are fired simultaneously (perhaps synchronously), either by sensory input or by internal association, feelings and behavior are elicited that are consistent with encountering or thinking about grandmother.

FIGURE SEGMENTATION

The perceptual system described in the previous section would work as long as only one figure is present in the visual field, which is rare in real life. As was true for olfaction, some segmentation process must be at work to ensure that neurons fired by background objects do not interfere with the pattern produced by the figure of interest.

Extrinsic factors may make a figure stand out. For example, figures of contrasting brightness, or ones that move, or flash (i.e. attention-getting figures) may stimulate the visual system strongly enough to suppress the effects of surrounding stimuli. This process is commonly classified as "bottom-up" attention.

---

[1]Versions of the program may be retrieved by anonymous ftp at the following URL: ftp://ego.psych.mcgill.ca/pub/milner

Except in infants, "top-down" attention is probably a more usual segmentation mechanism. As described for the olfactory system in chapter 3, once the neurons of an engram have become associated with a response plan or a motivational source of facilitation, their activity is increased when that source becomes active. One possibility (Milner, 1974) is that the increased engram activity facilitates corresponding sensory input via reciprocal paths that run parallel to the ascending activity. The feedback thus intensifies the sensory signal produced by the object of interest, resulting in an internally generated attention-getting effect.

Top down attention cannot occur, however, until an engram has been established for an object. Naive infants apparently must rely for figure segregation on extrinsic attention-getting mechanisms such as movement relative to the background, brightness, color, distance, and continuity of outline, factors that might give rise to synchronous firing of the implicated visual neurons (Milner, 1974).

It was known that neurons of the monkey visual system fire in irregular bursts during visual tasks (Wurtz, 1969), it thus seemed feasible that the bursts occurring in neurons fired by the same figure might be synchronous, but not in synchrony with the bursts of activity in neurons fired by other figures. Inputs from different parts of a figure converging on a neuron would therefore summate more effectively than inputs converging from different figures, ensuring that at any instant the visual network processes only one figure (Milner, 1974. p. 532).

As discussed in more detail later, a number of experiments now appear to show that synchronization is not limited to bursts of impulses, but applies also to individual impulses originating from parts of a single figure (Gray et al., 1989; Kreiter & Singer, 1996; Roelfsema, Engel, König, & Singer, 1997; Singer & Gray, 1995).

ACQUIRING TOP-DOWN ATTENTION

Convergence of the signals generated by simple figure elements can thus explain how an image that has moved or changed in size may continue to fire many of the same central neurons as before the change, and thus continue to be recognized. It does not immediately show how an active response plan can locate objects it needs to carry out a planned response. The plan must do that so that it can deliver attentional facilitation to neurons the object fires at an early level of the visual path, before convergence removes all localizing information. (Approximate localizing information for objects that have a fixed relation to a frame of reference, or map, may sometimes be stored as part of the representation of the object. We remember where our pockets and coat buttons are, for example, and can reach them without looking).

To understand how attentional facilitation may reach visual neurons that have precise information about the location of a goal object, it may help to continue the story of the dog and its food dish. Suppose food is regularly presented in a visually distinctive dish that the dog approaches in order to eat. Initially, curiosity or the smell of food may attract the dog. If the dog is attracted by the smell, neural activity corresponding to hunger and planning to eat presumably is present. That activity acquires associations with neurons fired by the sight of the food dish as the dog approaches it.

The dish stimulates many neurons throughout the dog's visual system. Some are specific to the position of its image on the dog's retinas whereas others are almost non-specific and fire whenever any object is seen. The sensory neurons that become most effectively associated with hunger and plans to approach a food dish are those that do not depend on any specific view of the dish but fire most of the time it is present.

Neurons whose activity is strongly correlated with the sight of the food dish, wherever it happens to be in the dog's field of view, obviously fire during a greater part of the dog's approach than neurons fired only by a specific view of the dish. They constitute a neural representation of the dish, and when it is in view, they are the neurons that acquire the strongest association with activity taking place at the time in the motivation/motor system.

As pointed out in chapter 3, it is this association that confers the designation of engram on these neurons. Until they have acquired an association, they are just some of the neurons fired by the situation. After the association, however, they may also be fired by association with a response plan or a specific motivation or emotion. By facilitating the corresponding sensory input and making it available to the motor system they contribute to the animal's purposive behavior. The association is assumed to take place in both directions, the association from the neurons of the response system to those of the engram being the more important for selective attention.

While the engram is being activated by its association with a motivated response plan, it ceases to be merely a latent trace and becomes an active working memory (Baddeley, 1986; Olton, Becker, & Handelmann, 1979). The associations ensure that whenever the dog becomes hungry or plans to seek food, engram neurons that previously fired during preparations to eat, including those representing the food dish, are facilitated.

LOCATING THE SOURCE NEURONS

If the food dish has a feature that is easily localized by the visual system, such as a characteristic color, the approach plan acquires associations with all visual neurons representing that color, including those with small fields at early levels of the visual cortex, such as V4 and V2. The position of the dish then can be deduced from those neurons, facilitated by the top-down feedback, that respond to the color of the dish.

In general, however, the target of attention may have no easily localizable feature, or the feature may not be unique to the target (e.g., the person wearing the red beret may not be who you thought she was). Furthermore, for some purposes the precision of localization furnished by such a feature might be inadequate. The enhancement of attention may need to reach the level of the individual line cells of V1 or V2 to provide the required accuracy of localization for a delicate manipulation. In such cases, attentional facilitation of the shape engram, and further feedback via the stimulus-equivalence circuit described earlier must be employed.

In that circuit, sensory input to the locus-insensitive engram neurons arrives from lower level sensory neurons that converge on them. These lower-level (more peripheral) sensory neurons, having smaller fields, are fired by specific images of the food dish, which depend on its location. Thus, although the engram neurons are themselves useless for accurate localization of the dish, they are in contact with more

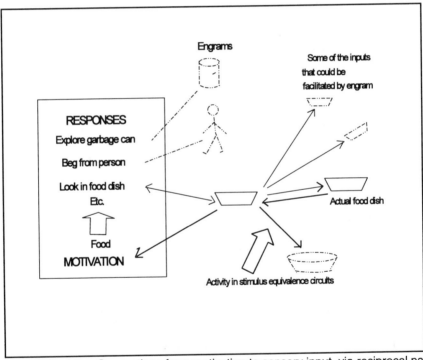

FIG. 4.3.   Connections from motivation to sensory input, via reciprocal paths.

peripheral neurons that carry the required spatial information. In the paper cited earlier (Milner 1974) it was postulated that the enhanced activity of the food-dish engram neurons is conveyed, as a facilitatory attention signal, to location-sensitive neurons earlier in the sensory path via the dense reciprocal connections to be found in all sensory cortex (Jones, 1974; Maunsell, 1995; Van Essen & Maunsell, 1983; von Bonin, Garol, & McCulloch, 1942).

Thus, attentional activity generated by the eating system fires engram neurons representing (among other things) food dishes, intensifying their firing if a food dish is present. The activated neurons in turn facilitate (via innate reciprocal connections) the peripheral sensory neurons that converge on them, intensifying the activity of any of the converging neurons that are firing (presumably because they are receiving input from a food dish at the time), as indicated in Fig. 4.3.

In this way, attention travels back through the chain of neurons being fired by the food dish until it reaches an early level, enhancing the signal from the food dish and partly suppressing other visual input. From these early levels the intensified food dish signal is distributed to all other visual areas, including the collicular, parietal, and frontal areas having to do with eye movement, locomotor guidance, and other aspects of motor control (Milner, 1974). Other visual input to these areas is attenuated or completely blocked. The attenuation of irrelevant cortical activity could be produced by a system that limits total cortical activity (Milner, 1957). The increased firing of facilitated neurons results in a compensatory inhibition of unfacilitated neurons.

Some support for this theory has been afforded by recent experiments of Desimone and his colleagues. In one experiment, Chelazzi et al. (1993) trained monkeys to make an eye movement at the appearance of a complex picture they had been shown a short time earlier. Two cue pictures were used, one that strongly activated a neuron in the inferotemporal cortex (good cue) and another that produced a weak response of the same neuron (poor cue). During the waiting period (no cue present), the neuron fired at a higher rate after the monkey had been shown the good cue than after it had been shown the poor one. At the end of the waiting period, both cues were presented at an equal distance from the fixation point and the monkey was rewarded for making an eye movement towards the cue it had been shown earlier.

When the two pictures appeared, the neuron's firing rate increased momentarily whether the good cue or the poor cue had been shown before, but within 200 ms the activity changed. If the good cue was correct, the increase in firing continued, even though no eye movement occurred for another 100 ms. If the poor cue was correct, the activity decreased and returned to a low level, even though the good picture still was in the field of the neuron. As attention (in advance of any adjustment of gaze) swiveled to the poor cue, the cortical activity produced by the (incorrect) good cue was suppressed.

During the initial presentation of the cue picture, the association between its engram neurons and the plan to fixate it appears to be boosted and remains high, facilitating the engram neurons during the waiting period. When the picture reappears, the facilitated neurons fire more vigorously, suppressing non-facilitated neurons in the neighborhood. Presumably the activity of corresponding retinotopic neurons at earlier visual levels is intensified, so that the location of the picture is relayed to the poised saccadic response, guiding it in the right direction.

Unfortunately, this experiment does not clarify how the activity of the retinotopic neurons is enhanced. Singer (1994) and his colleagues would say that the engram neurons responding to the correct picture fire synchronously with neurons fired by the same picture in the striate cortex, or perhaps the superior colliculus. Thus the fed-back impulses can be used to trigger a coincidence detector, which relays to the eye muscles only impulses from neurons fired by the correct target.

A somewhat similar suggestion was made in an unpublished postscript circulated with reprints of the paper on shape recognition cited earlier (Milner, 1974). The idea put forward involved a system in which coincidences of impulse bursts would be detected. Such a system would require considerably less temporal precision than one depending on the detection of synchronous single nerve impulses, but it would have a slower reaction time, and the effectiveness of segmentation would be reduced. The shape recognition system is quite robust. I doubted whether a system that depended on the coincidence of individual nerve impulses could be sufficiently precise to work reliably.

The experiments of Singer and a number of his colleagues (Engel, Roelfsema, Fries, Brecht, & Singer, 1997; Gray & Singer, 1989; König, Engel, & Singer, 1996; Kreiter & Singer, 1996; Singer, 1994; Singer & Gray, 1995) assuage those doubts to some extent. Apparently neurons fired in different areas of the brain by a single moving bar of light fire synchronously to within a millisecond or so, whereas when the same neurons are fired by two separate bars of light, their firing is uncorrelated. The same investigators have presented evidence showing that some cortical neurons have post-synaptic potentials that last only a few milliseconds, enabling them to discriminate against signals that are not accurately synchronized.

Although some compelling arguments support this hypothesis (König et al., 1996), it still has puzzling features, such as how synchrony can be maintained despite synaptic delays and the finite conduction speed of axons and dendrites. According to Ringo, Doty, Demeter, and Simard (1994), for example, visual impulses take approximately 20 ms to traverse the corpus callosum. This delay would make it difficult to achieve synchronization of impulses from an image that occupied both halves of the retina, which is the case for all but the smallest fixated objects.

The alternative described earlier, in which the fed-back facilitation is transmitted via recurrent visual paths, involves a more complicated feedback pathway but one that I would judge to be more robust. Moreover, there is strong anatomical evidence for complex reciprocal pathways at all levels of the sensory systems (Goldman-Racic, 1988; Jones, 1974; Maunsell, 1995; Van Essen & Maunsell, 1983). It is possible, however, that eventually some hybrid mechanism in which both timing and specific reciprocal pathways play a part will turn out to be involved.

SENSORY-MOTOR BINDING

As pointed out earlier, the whole point of transmitting attentional enhancement back to the retinotopic level is to provide the motor system with spatial information about the objects on which it has been set to operate. With synchrony of firing used as a binding agent, that objective is relatively easy to achieve. The enhanced activity of engram neurons is fed to coincidence-detecting neurons in the parietal visual path so that they relay only visual input pulses that are synchronous with the engram activity. Thus responses are guided only by information, including positional information, from the object being attended to.

Alternatively, attentional facilitation may be fed back from the active engram neurons to the primary visual cortex along a path parallel to the ascending path, enhancing the activity of neurons there that carry positional information. This information could then be delivered to the motor system via the dorsal visual path (Fig. 4.4). Unfacilitated neurons in the primary visual cortex are assumed to fire too feebly to have any direct influence on the motor system, but they still may act via the recognition path to influence response planning and changes of motivation.

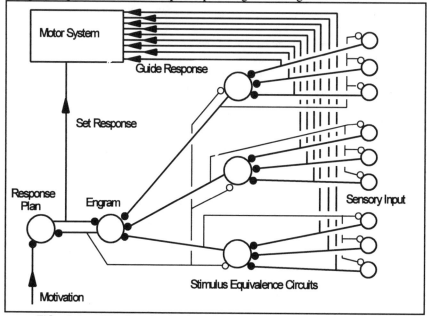

FIG. 4.4.   Attentional selection of sensory input for motor guidance.

Lesions of the parietal lobe are found to interfere with attention (Mesulam, 1983). Possibly they interfere with the conduction to the motor system of visual input that has been enhanced by attention. Damage to part of the ventral path does not interfere with all functions of the dorsal path according to the observations of Goodale and Milner (1992). These authors report on a patient who was quite unable to distinguish objects by their shape, but when asked to grasp an object, she did so perfectly normally, shaping the hand to the size of the object as soon as the reaching movement began.

When asked to demonstrate the size of the object using the thumb and finger, however, the patient was inaccurate and inconsistent. Thus, spatial information available at the visual input either reached the motor system or failed to do so, depending on the required response. Perhaps the determining factor is whether the response requires attention or is automatic.

MOTIVATION "LOCKING"

Although motivation may arise internally, as suggested earlier, this is not always the case. Perception of an object associated with food, for example, is liable to intensify the effect of mild food deprivation. Once aroused in this way, hunger focuses attention on the object, further increasing its effect on motivation. This positive feedback in the attentional process gives it some characteristics of an "attractor" circuit.

Unlike the cell-assembly type of feedback, however, attentional feedback does not, by itself, fire cortical neurons at the early levels of sensory paths; it merely lowers their thresholds by facilitating or disinhibiting them. In the absence of an appropriate stimulus, the feedback does not build up to cause reverberatory firing. If a stimulus corresponding to the attentional feedback is present, however, the neural activity it produces is amplified and becomes more resistant to interference from other inputs. The intensified activity continues either until the stimulus disappears, or until a different motivation changes the facilitatory feedback.

GENERALIZATION

As long as responses are rewarded, learned behavior proceeds according to the program described earlier. Our hypothetical dog associates its dish with food and is thereby motivated to approach it. Clearly, many of the neurons fired by the food dish must be fired also by other objects. Therefore the dog may approach an object sufficiently similar to the food dish, especially if highly motivated to eat.

Sometimes such generalizations pay off. The object that sufficiently resembles a food dish actually may contain food. If it does not, however, the association between the dish and food is weakened. The dog must learn to discriminate, a process discussed further in chapter 9 after the motivation system has been examined in greater detail.

MULTIPLE SOURCES OF ATTENTION

This account of how an intention selects needed stimuli is, of course, very incomplete . One obvious complication is that there may be a number of objects in the sensory field that could satisfy the intention but the motor system can cope with information from only one object at a time. In the visual system, when several objects associated with a response are in the field of view, the one closest to the fixation point produces the strongest signal and normally becomes the focus of attention. Other factors such as brightness, accessibility, or color also exert an influence.

If, for example, a person is looking for a yellow car, the search is made easier if attention is directed to yellow stimuli as well as car-shaped objects. The result is that facilitation is delivered simultaneously to all visual neurons that respond to yellow objects and those that respond to car shapes. Yellow cars elicit more feedback facilitation than cars of a different color or other yellow objects, and therefore attract the gaze.

The motivation system also has access to neurons, probably in the superior colliculus, that are connected to receptors at various distances and directions from central vision, allowing attentional facilitation of objects in different locations relative to the direction of gaze. If attention to a fixated object wanes for any reason, the input from another similar object may assume control of eye movements and produce a saccade in its own direction.

PHENOMENAL INTEGRATION

Neurons of the primary visual cortex distribute their outputs to areas specialized to process color, brightness, movement, depth, and the like (DeYoe & Van Essen, 1988). Nevertheless, when we perceive an object such as a cat, all its features (shape, color, motion, etc.) appear completely integrated.

How are the activities of neurons in many separate areas of the cortex so seamlessly bound together in the final percept? Trying to explain subjective phenomena such as this can get neuroscientists into deep water. Some discussions of "binding" are reminiscent of the Gestalt idea that the processes going on in the visual cortex are interpreted by the mind. A high-tech mind that scans all the visual areas and tries to determine which activities belong together in order to integrate them into a single percept, but still not easy to reconcile with neural activity..

Unfortunately, neural correlates of sensory experience are still a mystery (Block, 1996; Crick & Koch, 1990; Moscovitch, 1995; Vanderwolf, 1998). Awareness is known to be impaired or abolished by large lesions of sensory cortex, apparently without complete loss of response guidance in some cases (Goodale & Milner, 1992; Weiskrantz, 1990, 1997). However, such a lesion may cut off much of the sensory input to the rest of the cortex, so the information is not very helpful in localizing the effect.

Obtaining a verbal or other objective report of a percept depends on the motor system, which communicates sequentially. Therefore, although it is possible to confirm that different visual features are integrated in the percept of an object, it is impossible to determine the extent to which all the features are integrated simultaneously. What does seem highly likely is that the activities in different areas of the brain representing various features of a stimulus all acquire associations with some ongoing activity that serves to identify the episode during which the stimulus is present.

Earlier in this discussion I postulated that engram activity may be aroused by emotional and motivational circuits of the brain that were active during presentation of the stimulus. Thus, if a similar mental state subsequently arises, activity corresponding to the same combination of sensory features would be aroused. This explanation cannot be applied to the episodic memory of events passively observed, however. As discussed more fully in chapter 6, that seems to require a continuous background activity, probably having markers for time and location, to which other sensory events can become linked.

One theory of feature integration is that the outputs of neurons fired synchronously in different visual areas, combine through coincidence detectors to fire these episodic memory neurons (König et al., 1996; Singer, 1994). An alternative, discussed earlier, is that attention (bottom-up or top-down) intensifies the activity evoked in the primary visual cortex by an object. The selected signal is then distributed to all the specialized visual areas. These areas therefore receive, more or less simultaneously, an intensified input from the object in question that overrides other inputs to the areas. As in the synchronous-firing theory, these separate activities are postulated to converge on episodic memory neurons and acquire reciprocal associations with them.

Although we have the subjective impression of seeing an integrated image, eye witnesses are notoriously inaccurate. To answer detailed questions, such as what fruit are in the bowl, or what color are the man's socks, attention must be directed separately to specific features. Puzzles that require observation of small differences between two similar pictures demonstrate how little detail can be stored at a single glance. Children with eidetic imagery are a possible exception to the rule. They reputedly are able to remember a great deal more detail, possibly by using an unusual type of synaptic change.

STIMULUS EQUIVALENCE IN AUDITION

The location of a source of sound does not greatly influence the pattern of auditory receptor activity, though it may affect intensity and phase, variables that are especially important to animals that hunt in the dark or in murky waters. Sound frequency is the main parameter that influences receptor firing. Frequency ratios are more important for meaning than absolute frequency.

If sounds of different frequency are concurrent their ratios define the quality (or timbre) of the sound, if sequential the ratios define a tune. Both of these aspects of sounds are useful in identifying its source and both exhibit stimulus equivalence. The voice of a friend is recognizable, no matter what she is saying, as is the bray of a trombone, no matter what it is playing. A song is easily recognized whether it is sung by a tenor or a soprano.

The principle of convergence that was suggested to explain stimulus equivalence in the visual system could also explain these examples of auditory stimulus equivalence. If the outputs of all neurons that are fired by the combination of sounds having the same frequency ratio, say two to one, converge on another neuron, that neuron would be fired by all octaves.

The major complication with audition, however, as mentioned in chapter 1, is that interpreting a stimulus usually requires accumulating information over time. Time, unlike space cannot be retraced. There is no moving back and forth through time. Time cannot be stored for later use; temporal sequences must be converted into spatial sequences for storage and later regeneration.

The brain is not exempt from this constraint. Representations of words and other auditory input must involve these time - space, followed by space - time, conversions. The problem of representing and retrieving temporal order is the subject of the next chapter.

SUMMARY

Primitive animals use smell to recognize and evaluate objects at a distance and decide whether to approach, avoid or ignore them. Objects in close proximity are investigated tactually to discover what should be done with them. Vision can perform both of these functions more effectively. A ventral visual pathway augments the olfactory system, indicating what a stimulus is for, and a dorsal visual pathway provides information used to manipulate objects (Sakata, Taira, Kusunoki, Murata, & Tanaka, 1997).

An object usually has only a single distinctive smell, but it can present innumerable visual images. Visual input is influenced by such features as distance, size, retinal position, angle of view, and orientation, which have little to do with the identity of the stimulus. The ventral pathway is designed to discard, by successive convergences, information that does not contribute to identification, retaining a pattern that provides only a functional description of the object.

If the animal decides to make a response to the object, however, some of the discarded information is required to control the response. Actions are guided mainly by visual information passing along the dorsal route. The problem is to ensure that only information from the object inducing the action is delivered to the motor system. One suggestion is that visual impulses generated by a single object are synchronized throughout the nervous system, allowing the use of coincidence detectors to ensure that only impulses originating from an object selected for action by a ventral-path engram are admitted to the dorsal path.

The objection to this suggestion is that even a slight error of synchronization would produce chaos in the response mechanism. An alternative possibility is that engrams eliciting an action generate an attention signal that is passed back via reciprocal fibers parallel to the ascending ventral path, until it reaches the level at which the dorsal path branches off. Only visual impulses intensified by the descending attention signal are admitted to the dorsal path.

Both theories can account for what sometimes is known as the binding problem. Enhanced activity of retinotopic sensory neurons when the feature to which they are responding receives attention, affects all the visual areas to which they project. Thus, attending to a chrysanthemum, for example, intensifies the firing of neurons representing orange in the visual area for color, or paying attention to red intensifies the activity of neurons fired by the shape of a red rose. Although we can imagine without too much difficulty how the firing of certain neurons can allow us to report that we see red, for example, it would be foolish to claim that we have any idea how the firing of neurons causes us to experience sensations.

In the theory advanced here, intentions are not always dependent on external influences. As long as the central activity corresponding to an intention continues, the sensory system is sensitized to stimuli that have been associated with the intended behavior on previous occasions. If one of those stimuli is detected, its input is intensified so that it releases and guides the planned response.

The auditory system resembles the visual system in that it interprets the input from the ear along a number of dimensions in specialized brain areas. The outputs of the two ears are combined to give directional information; harmonics are combined to give information about the tonal quality of the sound, and so on. As in the other sensory systems, attention normally is directed to whatever type of analysis is relevant to the motivation of the listener.

5 Temporal Order

The human genetic code is very similar to that of other great apes. No doubt some of the difference is responsible for the superior strength and stamina of most non-human apes, but much of the rest must explain why, while most species of ape struggle to survive, humans have expanded their range to most of the earth's surface and beyond, and are well on the way to making the planet an uncomfortable, if not impossible, place on which to live.

A few percent of the genetic code of an ape represents an enormous amount of information, but the difference between the current lifestyle of human beings and that of the chimpanzee is incomparably greater than that between chimpanzee and bears, for example, whose DNA exhibits a much greater difference. What did those mutations of primate DNA do to produce this enormous gap? I am probably not alone in suspecting that speech played a significant role.

Most birds and mammals must have patterns of neural activity that correspond to significant stimuli, but it is questionable how detailed or specific the correspondences are. We humans attach great importance to our ability to verbalize experiences. The research on amnesia provides many examples of patients diagnosed as amnesic because they are incapable of recalling (or declaring) an experience which nevertheless did leave a permanent trace as shown by subsequent behavior (Schacter, 1994). Animals can indicate what they remember only by non- verbal behavior, so it is possible that they resemble amnesic patients as regards what they can consciously remember.

If, as suggested in chapter 3, intentions (response plans) play a mediating role in the association of concepts, the availability of names for most of our concepts must greatly facilitate thinking. A name, after all, is a response associated with a particular concept or group of concepts. The response plan is associated closely with the sounds we make (every time a word is pronounced it also is heard), permitting chains of associations to develop.

Words allow us to communicate with ourselves as well as with others. Using words, we are able to rehearse complex plans that involve abstract concepts and absent stimuli without overt performance of the contemplated responses. Apparently words can be substituted for other more energetic responses. The neural basis of such a powerful tool surely deserves more attention than it has been accorded in the past.

SEQUENTIAL RESPONSES

Like most responses, words are produced by an ordered sequence of muscle contractions. The problem of how we store and recall temporal order extends far beyond the learning of words, but the mechanism for dealing with rapid sequences of events, such as those involved in the production and understanding of speech and music, is of particular interest. In 1951 Lashley delivered a landmark address with the title: *The Problem of Serial Order in Behavior.* He said:

> I have chosen to discuss the problem of temporal integration here, not with the expectation of offering a satisfactory physiological theory to account for it, but because it seems to me both the most important and the most neglected problem of cerebral physiology. (Lashley, 1951, p. 112)

Although temporal order is somewhat less neglected now than in Lashley's time (Elman, 1990; Hopfield & Tank, 1989), it is still not a problem that attracts a great deal of research. Because it is primarily a motor function, serial order is somewhat peripheral to the main thrust of neuropsychology. Besides, few if any of us remember a time when we could not speak, so we are tempted to think that learning words is simple, perhaps a straightforward case of stimulus - response association.

The study of language is a mainstay of cognitive psychology, but the treatment rarely descends to such fundamental aspects as learning to recognize and pronounce words, although (Elman, 1990) developed a connectionist approach to the problem, using a dynamic form of storage. I question the physiological plausibility of Elman's model, however, for reasons similar to those raised in the discussion of Hebb's cell assembly (chapter 3).

Understanding the neural mechanism involved in speaking is of general interest because learning to pronounce a word is like learning to imitate any response that involves a rapid sequence of movements performed in a particular order (playing an instrument, for example, or golf). A fundamental question arises in trying to explain how we learn to pronounce a word. How are the order and timing of the movements in a sequence recorded and stored.

First, it must be acknowledged that a single presentation of a sequence, if not attended to, becomes inaccessible in a few seconds. A word must be pronounced repeatedly, at least subvocally, to prolong storage. To remember the pronunciation of a word (or any other complex sequence of movements) from one day to the next, the sequence must be rehearsed a number of times while it is "fresh in the mind." Nevertheless, it is remarkable that a series of sounds, perhaps including repetitions of an identical sound, can be stored neurally, even for a short period, after only a single presentation.

To be useful, a newly learned word must acquire meaning and be recognized when it is heard again. If the word is to be reproduced, and not merely used as an informative stimulus, a permanent motor sequence for pronouncing it must be established and associated with the meaning. It should be clear from all this that although learning to speak may be effortless, the neural mechanisms for even the most basic use of words cannot be simple.

ENGRAMS INVOLVING TEMPORAL ORDER

The mechanism for merely recognizing words and other sounds, without the capacity to reproduce them, is perhaps the most simple introduction to the major conundrums posed by response learning. The ability to associate words or sounds with some action or emotional tone can be demonstrated in young infants who cannot yet talk, and it is a skill they share with many animals. (House cats typically ignore verbal attempts to limit their autonomy, but they have no trouble with important sounds like those made by a can-opener, or refrigerator door). Only a few species, mostly birds and, of course, our own, can learn to mimic the sounds they hear.

The trouble with auditory stimuli is that they involve the time dimension. This is true of other stimuli, of course, but whereas visual stimuli make use of massively parallel communication channels to transfer meaningful spatial patterns very rapidly, the temporal component of an auditory pattern normally is essential for its meaning. Changing the order of the components changes the meaning completely. A cat is not the same as a tack, and both are different from an act.

To recognize the word "cat," therefore, we must store not only representations of the three component phonemes, but also their order of arrival. To appreciate a drawing, we do not need to know the order in which the artist drew the lines, but to recognize a tune or a word, it is essential to experience and remember the order, and often the timing, of the sounds. I do not believe anyone has yet discovered how this is achieved, but we can probably make better-informed guesses today than Lashley (1951) was able to do on the basis of 1940s neurophysiology.

Presumably, the permanent neural representation of a word is based on changes in synaptic effectiveness. The three sound components of the word "cat," the K, the A, and the T, must each be represented by a pattern of modified synapses, but the engram for the complete word must be more than just the sum of those patterns. Otherwise "cat" would be indistinguishable from "tack,"

The idea that a stimulus initiates persistent firing of some cortical neurons was introduced in chapter 3. The first phoneme of a word triggers such a persisting activity, which then facilitates and inhibits other

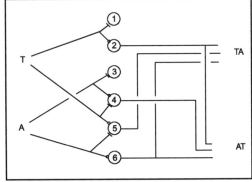

FIG. 5.1.   Neural representation of sound order.

cortical neurons, influencing the pattern of firing and synaptic change elicited by the second phoneme. The combined after-effects of the first two sounds then influence the pattern of firing and synaptic change produced by a third, and so on (see Lewicki & Konishi, 1995).

The final result is that the pattern of cortical activity set up by the complete word differs from a pattern composed of the sum of its separate elementary components. This is illustrated by the diagram (Fig. 5.1), in which, to simplify things, only two sounds are considered, each of them temporarily exciting two neurons and inhibiting two, with some overlap. If T occurs first, it fires neurons 2 and 5 and inhibits 1 and 4. A following sound, A, is able to fire only neuron 6 because 4 is inhibited. If A occurs first, it fires both 4 and 6 and inhibits 3 and 5. Thus T can fire only neuron 2.

The resulting output codes resemble those produced by any other type of stimulus. They are not themselves sequential, but they incorporate the order in which the components arrived. To match a word engram, auditory input must follow the same sequence as the word that originally produced the engram. If we assume that each of the neurons in Fig. 5.1 represents a group of neurons with a range of different rates of recovery from stimulation, then some record of the interval between the sounds would be stored also.

PRONUNCIATION

The preceding hypothesis is plausible and it may even bear some (much simplified) resemblance to the way the brain solves the word recognition problem, but it cannot explain our ability to pronounce words. Although the pattern of changed synapses represents the sounds and their order of occurrence, the order cannot easily be extracted from it.

Thus, facilitating the group of neurons (via a motivation signal for example) would not cause the response plans for the sounds to fire in the correct order. It might try to fire them all at once, or it might produce some entirely different response. A more complicated mechanism must be invoked to account for the correct order of sound production during learned pronunciation of a word.

ASSOCIATION OF SOUND WITH RESPONSE

The first requirement for mimicking a word (or other sound) is to be able to link the sound with a motor activity. Motor systems become active even before animals are born or hatched. Infants have an inborn tendency to mimic facial gestures such as yawning and tongue protrusion (Meltzoff & Moore, 1989) and, when frequently spoken to, they babble while mimicking the sounds and mouth movements of the adult. Infants whose deaf parents use sign language do not babble, but mimic the hand gestures of those around them (Petitto & Marentette, 1991).

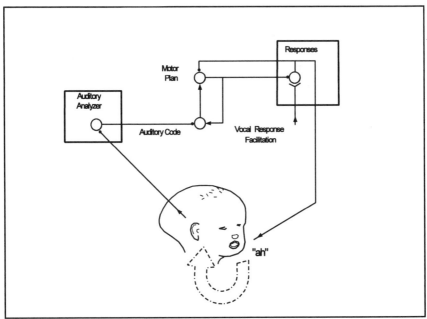

FIG. 5.2.   Sensory motor association during infant babbling.

As they babble, babies learn the sensory consequences of their vocal responses. A certain motor activity produces the sound "ah," for example, which stimulates the auditory system and fires a pattern of sensory neurons corresponding to that sound. Frequent repetition of the activity results in an association (Fig. 5.2) between the pattern of sensory firing and the motor-system activity responsible for producing the sound. (That association also may have an innate basis). Subsequently, by way of these connections, hearing a pronounceable sound facilitates the motor neurons capable of producing it. Depending on motivational activity, the infant may ignore the sound, interpret it as information, or attempt to mimic it.

Concurrent internal states also acquire associations with the sound engrams. Then, not only do sounds evoke motivational and emotional states, but arousal of those states by other means elicits corresponding vocalization via their association with the motor apparatus.

Further insight into the neural processes involved in language acquisition derive from research on people profoundly deaf from birth who have learned to use sign language (Petitto et al., 1997). Cerebral blood flow was measured using positron emission tomography (PET) in native users of American or Quebec sign language and a control group of subjects with normal hearing who did not know sign language. All the subjects showed increased blood flow in the left prefrontal cortex (Broca's area) when viewing or generating words, but not when exposed to isolated letters. It seems that the area is important for language, irrespective of the motor activity required to produce it.

Some experiments of Rizzolatti and his colleagues (e.g. Rizzolatti & Arbib, 1998) also are relevant to the neural mechanism of imitation. These investigators found neurons in the region of the monkey frontal cortex thought to be homologous to the human area for speech (Broca's area) that fired when monkeys were engaged in activities involving the hand or mouth. The neural firing was correlated with an action, such as grasping, biting, or tearing, not with a particular movement.

What is exciting about Rizzolatti's observations is that some of these neurons also fired when the monkey saw someone else performing the same action. Clearly, the animals must have neural representations (or plans) of activities they engage in frequently, and these have connections to sensory input that accompanies the activities. It is not clear whether the connections are learned or innate, but the similar localization of language areas in deaf and hearing people (Petitto et al., 1997), and the ability of very young infants to imitate facial gestures that it would be impossible for them to see when they make them themselves, indicate a strong genetic component to imitation, including imitation of speech movements and sounds.

IMITATION OF SOUND SEQUENCES

So far, the sounds imitated by the infant have been assumed to be elemental, not involving sequences of vocal activity. When infants can produce simple sounds at will, however, they soon begin to arrange them in sequences to reproduce words they hear. This requires the order of the elementary sounds to be stored in a form readily accessible to the motor system. Rehearsal of the sequence then is able to establish a more permanent record of the word.

Once a number of words have been learned, a similar (possibly the same) sequencing device may be used to store and reproduce strings of words. In this way a telephone number, heard just once, can be stored for a short time until dialed. Frequent repetition of the number establishes a permanently stored sequence that can be triggered by the engram of an object or name associated with the telephone number.

There must be a close relationship between the engram for recognizing a word and the dynamic motor circuit for pronouncing it. Probably it is significant that in human beings and some other apes rhythmic sounds can provoke rhythmic muscle contractions that range from almost imperceptible twitching to uninhibited leaping about, further implicating the motor system in the interpretation of temporal order.

NEURAL CIRCUITS FOR MOTOR SEQUENCES

Before speculating on how motor performances are learned, it might be useful to review what is known about mechanisms for producing unlearned motor sequences. The butterfly emerges from its chrysalis and within minutes flies off in the deceptive flip-flop manner characteristic of its species. The newborn caribou stands up and joins the trek of the migrating herd almost immediately. Flying and walking involve intricate temporal sequences of muscle activation. The innate neural connections of almost every animal must include circuits capable of generating some form of locomotor sequence.

Székely (1968) suggested a simple oscillatory circuit consisting of an odd number of inhibitory neurons connected in a ring (Fig. 5.3), which appears to be the basis of at least some repetitive movements in animals. Stent, Kristan, Friesen, Ort, Poon, and Calabrese (1978) identified such a circuit consisting of five neurons while recording the activity of identified neurons in the ganglia of the ventral cord of the leech. The circuit was connected to the swimming muscles of the leech and presumably would have produced swimming in the intact animal.

With no input, the neurons are, of course, quiescent. But if the whole loop is subjected to a steady excitatory bombardment, the neuron with the lowest threshold (or perhaps the one closest to the source of excitation) starts to fire, preventing the next neuron in the loop from firing. Thus the third neuron in the chain receives no inhibition and is free to fire, as are all the odd-numbered neurons.

Because the number of neurons in the loop is odd, the last one is not inhibited,

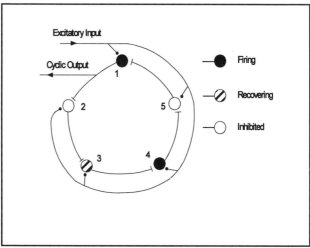

FIG. 5.3.   Inhibitory loop for producing cyclic bursts of neural firing.

and when it fires it inhibits the first. This releases the second neuron from inhibition, allowing it to fire and inhibit the third. When the inhibition reaches the last neuron, the first is released again, and so around the chain. In this way, waves of activity run around the loop as long as the activating input is maintained. As each neuron fires, it produces a contraction of the swimming muscle to which it is connected.

After each neuron stops firing, its inhibitory effect on the next neuron takes a little time to decay, so the interval between the cessation of firing in one neuron and the onset of firing in the next depends on the intensity of the excitatory input. The stronger the input to the loop, the sooner each neuron breaks through the decaying inhibitory aftereffect, and the faster the leech swims.

It seems likely that there are brainstem and spinal circuits in vertebrates that use a similar principle to generate innate sequential patterns (Grillner, Wallén, Brodin, & Lansner, 1991). Loops and chains of inhibitory neurons also are observed in the cerebral parts of the vertebrate motor system (chapter 8), suggesting that they play a role in circuits for learned sequential behavior.

Sequences are the speciality of the motor system. Almost every action involves the firing of muscles in a predetermined order. Many of the circuits for producing the required order are innate. The motoneurons for the muscles involved in swallowing, for example, fire in the correct sequence even if the muscles themselves have been paralyzed to prevent proprioceptive feedback (Doty & Bosma, 1956).

In some cases, order is imposed by the environment. A person must grasp a doorknob before turning it, and turn it before pushing the door, but other learned motor sequences are too fast to be cued by environmental feedback. Typing, playing a musical instrument, and speaking are in that category. We are faced with the problem of explaining how such learned sequential programs are acquired.

LEARNING A NEW WORD

Once children have learned to speak, typically they can repeat a word they have just heard for the first time. This is something a tape recorder also can do, but obviously not using the same technique. The tape recorder can repeat only what it has "heard". It does not have a voice of its own. The human speech mechanism reconstructs the word from a number of familiar sounds: individual phonemes or groups of phonemes that occur in words already known. The auditory system recognizes the component sounds, records the order in which they are heard, and on demand feeds that information to the motor system so that it produces its own versions of the sounds in the same order.

The first time a word is heard, the stored information decays within seconds if it does not attract attention. If the auditory input activates vocal motor plans for mimicking the sounds, the information is re-stored for a further few seconds, even if the vocal output is suppressed, a process known as silent rehearsal. Each time the motor plans fire in this way, the stored information about the order of the sounds becomes more firmly fixed, after which, when triggered by an appropriate signal, the word can be pronounced hours or days later. If frequently used, the sequence that produces the word becomes permanently established.

The crucial process that makes such motor learning possible is the immediate storage of a sequence of events. When we hear a new word or a short tune, it lingers in the memory for a few seconds. This phenomenon requires that the temporal relationships among a series of stimuli be stored and recalled. If identical stimuli in any modality are presented at intervals, they can be distinguished temporally from each other. They clearly do not stimulate entirely identical patterns of neurons, or this would not be possible.

The temporal pattern can be recalled and used to control motor activity. In fact, the stored pattern has many characteristics of a response plan. It can be turned on by appropriate motivation; the remembered rhythm can be speeded up or slowed down, the beats counted, and so on.

If, as seems certain, the pronunciation of long words must be learned, temporal order must be stored at least briefly at the sensory level as a basis for rehearsal. The instant replay feature works best when the listener attends to the material to be recalled, but it also works when attention is otherwise engaged. A remark heard by a reader engrossed in a book may be recalled and understood seconds later after attention has been switched to the auditory mode. As Broadbent (1956) demonstrated, if two lists of words are presented simultaneously, one to each ear, the listener attends to one list and remembers it, then can switch attention to the trace of the other list and recall it almost as successfully.

NEURAL TIMERS

A basic requirement for the perception of temporal order is a timer. Time usually is measured in terms of the distance traveled by something moving at a steady rate. Alternatively, it can be estimated from observations of physical or chemical changes such as evaporation, fermentation, combustion, cooling, and so on.

Artifacts for storing temporal sequences invariably convert time into space, usually in the form of a moving film or tape. The recording is played back to recover the temporal relationships. Biological timers contain no tapes, but transient effects of a stimulus could spread with time from neuron to neuron, or possibly even within the dendritic tree of a neuron.

Some years ago the suggestion was made that neurons fired by a sequence of events acquire a temporary association with neurons connected in a chain so that they always fire in the same order, analogously to a tape recorder (Milner, 1961a). One of the many practical difficulties with this idea is finding a way to start the chain firing at the right place to recall a specific item of needed information.

A more plausible alternative to the moving neural trace is the fading trace. There is no doubt that changes take place in neurons after synaptic activation, but it is not obvious how these might be used to recover the temporal aspect of such a trace. The longer the delay, the weaker the trace is likely to have become, a circumstance that would favor a "last in, first out" reordering of traces during retrieval.

A possible way around that problem would be to have the sensory events potentiate the synapses from a source of clock pulses to neurons of the "echo" trace, as described in chapter 3, but then immediately inhibit the trace neuron (or a neuron that the trace neuron excites). If the inhibitory trace decays more rapidly than the potentiation, the neuron will start to fire again after a certain length of time.

To recall a sequence represented by such a trace, the system is probed by an attention signal of such intensity that it just neutralizes the inhibition that suppresses the neurons storing the first sound of the sequence. Then, as the inhibitory traces blocking neurons storing the later sounds decay to the level of the excitatory probe input, the stored sounds are released in their correct sequence. As each neuron fires again, it restores both its potentiation and the inhibitory trace that counteracts the potentiation, and the cycle starts again.

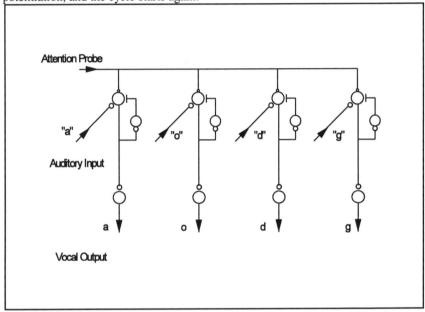

FIG. 5.4.   Immediate retrieval of auditory sequence by attention probe.

For example, in Fig. 5.4, the word dog fires the "d" neuron, which immediately inhibits itself. (The vocal output of the listener is turned off during auditory input, so the "d" is not pronounced.) The same process is repeated for the "o" and "g" neurons as the rest of the word is heard. If a stream of activity then is delivered along the probe axon, the "d" neuron fires first because its recovery from the aftereffect of the inhibition is furthest advanced. The "o" and the "g" fire later, as their thresholds fall to the critical level.

In this model, if a phoneme occurs more than once in a word, the second occurrence finds the neurons that fired previously are inhibited. This suggests that backup neurons must exist that are not fired by the first occurrence of a sound, but are available to be fired by a second or subsequent occurrence. Perhaps the elevated thresholds of some neurons are reduced by the first occurrence, preparing them to be fired later if the sound recurs.

Alternatively, because of random threshold fluctuations, perhaps only a fraction of the neurons that receive input from a particular stimulus (and have connections with the corresponding vocal output) are fired at any single presentation of a stimulus. Thus, even though an earlier occurrence of a phoneme leaves some of the neurons inhibited for a time, there would still be a supply of unfired neurons available if the phoneme is repeated later in the sequence. The capacity of the short-term memory is quite small, and not many English words have more than six or seven syllables. If an attempt is made to store a second new word or tune, it overwrites the first.

A dynamic verbal memory, with characteristics similar to those attributed to this model, is impaired by lesions of the left posterior temporal and parietal cortex (Warrington & Shallice, 1969). Any information stored there has to find a more permanent home if it is not to disappear as soon as attention wanders.

As a way of permanently storing a sequence, neurons fired by the first phoneme could establish synaptic connections with some neurons fired by the second phoneme, and those fired by the second phoneme could do the same with neurons fired by a third, and so on. As Lashley (1951) pointed out, however, this method ceases to be useful as soon as another word starting with the same phoneme is encountered.

Linking response elements from an unselected pool to form a chain is feasible only as a temporary measure. It is useless for permanent storage. For temporary storage the synaptic change must be reversed after a short time, leaving the chain free for another sequence. Lashley recognized that permanent storage of similar elements in different sequences requires that the elements be preselected from a larger pool by some activity unique to the word being learned, by the engram of the word, in fact.

For example, when the word "cat" is being pronounced, a nonsequential engram for cat, established as described earlier, could facilitate a small fraction of all the response neurons capable of generating the "k," "a," and "t" sounds. This allows the selected neurons to acquire associations with each other and produce their sounds in the correct order to pronounce the word cat. Being selected, the neurons neither interfere with other sequences that include the same sounds, such as cab, nor do they receive interference from other overlapping sequences.

But there is another snag. The first time a word or other sound sequence is heard, no engram for it can exist until the end of the sequence is reached. By that time, the individual sounds have disappeared into thin air. This is why it is necessary to preserve the order of the sounds in a temporary neural "echo" until the engram is available to select the elements for a permanent trace.

Once the engram is established and active, it allocates a select group of phoneme neurons to store the response plan. Although the word to be stored is no longer present, and its engram does not retain information about the order of sounds, the selected neurons can be associated with each other in the correct order by repeated activation of the transiently stored "echo trace." The neurons selected for this purpose are not selected by any other word engram, so their associations with each other are not degraded or overwritten by other words that use the same phonemes.

Thus, after someone hears the word "dog" for the first time and plans to pronounce it, the information is stored in the form of transient inhibitory traces by groups of neurons associated with the production of the sounds "d," "o," and "g." Under the influence of an excitatory input, the neurons start to fire in sequence as they recover in turn from the inhibition. It would not have been possible to select the neurons constituting the transient trace of "dog" because the sounds following the "d" were unknown, the word never having been heard before. Thus, although the trace can persist for a time if undisturbed, it would be displaced by any subsequent word.

Once it has been established, the dog engram contains or can recruit small samples of neurons representing the phonemes that it is storing, which are then associated with each other in the correct order by the firing of the temporary echo. It is indeed probable that they are neurons participating in the echo that are selected and removed from a general pool by the action of the engram. Thus a group of "d" neurons acquire associations with selected groups of "o" and "g" neurons, and selected "o" neurons are associated with "g" neurons.

In this way, the required sequence is stored by a chain of associations, but the neurons permitted to join the chain are preselected by the engram of the word. The engram for "dig" preselects a set of "d" neurons different from those selected by the engram for "dog," so each can have its own associations with following sounds.

Thus, to store a permanent record requires a two-stage process in which the sounds establish a unique nonsequential engram and at the same time assemble a temporary sequential trace. The engram then is used to restrict the sample of neurons that can participate in a permanent motor chain capable of pronouncing the word. This chain is built up during repeated rehearsal of the temporarily stored sequence.

The children of deaf parents, who learn sign language, must use a similar mechanism except that they must associate visual stimuli with neurons that activate their arm and hand muscles (Petitto & Marentette, 1991; Petitto et al., 1997). Learning to write involves much the same process, with the added complication of translation between auditory and visual information.

SUMMARY

The ability to learn sequences of responses is about the most useful talent an animal can have. It is particularly important for human beings because language depends on it, and there can be little doubt that language facilitates and enriches thinking.

Sequences introduce a new factor into learning. Not only must the nervous system be changed by an event, but the timing of the event in relation to other events also must be recorded. An early theory held that the elements of a sequence form a chain of associations, the first evoking the second, the second evoking the third, and so on. The obvious flaw in this theory is that there are only a few phonemic elements and they enter into very many combinations. Thus, associations acquired during the learning of one word would soon be overpowered by a multitude of new associations as other words are encountered.

Sequences that contain the same elements in different orders can produce different recognition codes because the neural activity produced by later events is influenced by the aftereffects of prior events. Thus, if the same events occur in a different order, they will fire different patterns of neurons. Each word, therefore, generates a unique engram that, like engrams in other modalities, is associated with a meaning. However, this engram cannot readily provide the sequential information needed by the motor system to pronounce the word.

Lashley (1951) cited the example of common typing errors, such as the reversal of letters, to support the idea that a representation of the whole word is active throughout the production of its letter or phonemic sequence, and that some other process is responsible for the order. He did not specify how the representation of the whole word is generated, however, nor how it interacts with the sequencing process.

Even if a word can establish its engram on a single exposure, the engram cannot be complete until the whole word has been heard, by which time the individual elements are history. There must be some mechanism for storing the temporal relations of the elements, at least for a short time, so that both the engram and the complete sequence of elements can be active simultaneously.

The neurons participating in the temporary store do not acquire associations with each other. Each independently turns itself off immediately after it receives an input, and recovers after a fixed interval, resulting in a sort of virtual time base. As the inhibitory traces fade, the earliest input to be stored is the first to be released in response to facilitation delivered to all the storage neurons.

To store the sequence permanently, the engram for the word is used to facilitate a restricted sample of vocal response neurons at the time the temporarily stored sequence is being recalled. Then each sound in the sequence is associated with only a select few of the corresponding response neurons. In this way, because different engrams facilitate different groups of neurons, it is possible to associate a single sound with many different preceding sounds, depending on the word being learned.

6 Memory

All physical systems store their past experiences. Rocks retain the heat of the sun after it has set. The magnetism and crystal structure of minerals reveal the conditions under which they were formed, and machines wear out or rust. Inanimate objects rarely benefit from the information they store; the reverse is more likely to be true. The cumulative effect of all those revolutions finally lands an internal combustion engine on the scrap heap. Animals, however, have evolved methods of benefiting from the effects of their experiences.

SYNAPTIC PLASTICITY

The aftereffects of chemical reactions usually are obvious, and may last indefinitely. Living organisms are highly active cauldrons of chemical reactions so there is no lack of material to be tapped for information about their past. It is now widely believed that memories are based primarily on activity-induced changes in the effectiveness of synapses. In fact, many processes with different time courses have been observed to affect the functioning of neurons after synaptic activation.

Exposure to transmitter substance changes a neuron in many ways. Some of the changes are caused by the flow of ions through channels that are opened when a transmitter binds to certain membrane-spanning receptor proteins. Other receptor molecules have no ion channels, but the intracellular part of the molecule is coupled to guanosine triphosphate binding protein (G-protein) that is activated when a transmitter binds to the extracellular part of the receptor. The activated G-protein is coupled to other enzymes that produce cyclic adenosine monophosphate (cAMP), cyclic guanosine monophosphate (cGMP), diacylglycerol (DAG), or other second messengers that may induce a multitude of intracellular changes.

Some second messengers, for example, bind to the intracellular end of ion channels to either open or close the channel, or they may activate protein kinases that also can open or close ion channels (Routtenberg, 1986). In addition, they may phosphorylate proteins, causing them to synthesize nitric oxide or carbon monoxide. These volatile products diffuse freely through cell membranes and are thought to provide communication between postsynaptic neurons and the presynaptic terminals that end on them (Zhuo, Kandel, & Hawkins, 1994).

Ion channels opened directly by transmitter substances usually remain open for no more than a few milliseconds, and the ions are soon expelled by other membrane-spanning proteins (ion pumps). When calcium ions enter, however, they act directly on other ion channels, opening or closing them. Calcium ions also play a major role in the chemistry of the cell.

It has been known for many years that calcium is needed for the release of transmitter substance from axon terminals, and for other types of secretion (Knight, von Grafenstein, & Athayde, 1989). Calcium ions also bind to protein kinase (Routtenberg, 1985), protein phosphatase, calmodulin, and calpain to activate these enzymes, which then act alone or in conjunction with other second messengers to produce a great variety of internal changes, one of which is to modify gene expression (Meberg, Barnes, McNaughton, & Routtenberg, 1993). The consequences of gene activation are legion, including changes in metabolism and, of course, consolidation of changes in synaptic efficacy.

Because protein synthesis takes place mostly in cell nuclei, and as there may be as many as 30,000 synapses on a single cortical neuron, the question arises as to how a newly synthesized protein for consolidating learning finds the synapses at which it should act. One theory is that molecules in the vicinity of recently activated synapses are marked in some way, perhaps by phosphorylation, to attract the newly synthesized substance to its target (Bear, 1997; Frey & Morris, 1997). As shall be seen, disturbing the brain can permanently eliminate memories less than about a minute old. This may be how long it takes to produce the markers and the enzymes that activate genes. It may be several hours before the new protein is synthesized and incorporated into the synapse.

A great deal has been learned about the complex enzymatic reactions that occur during neural transmission (Milner et al., 1998), more than it would be appropriate to present in detail here. So many factors influence the final outcome that the information can serve only as a basis for speculation about the mechanisms of synaptic plasticity involved in memory. The most important message for psychologists and neural model builders is that processes so far discovered, including the production of second messengers, phosphorylation of enzymes, and the modification of gene expression, can explain changes in synaptic effectiveness that endure for a few fractions of a second up to the lifetime of the subject, though the signaling cascades involved in any particular memory process are not yet known in most cases.

EARLY RESEARCH

Scientific study of learning and memory began in the late 19th century at the time when Ebbinghaus (1885) was performing his pioneering experiments on the recall of nonsense syllables. The nonsense syllable technique was used later by Müller and Pilzecker (1900) to study the effect of activity interposed between learning and the testing of retention. Not surprisingly, the investigators found that the best condition for retention was no interposed distraction. Learning a second list of nonsense syllables interfered with retention of the first. The disruptive effect became more severe as the similarity of the lists increased and the interval between the learning of the two lists decreased.

The methodology of these experiments is not beyond criticism, but Müller and Pilzecker's (1900) explanation for the effect (i.e. that a memory trace needs time to become "fixed") ushered the notion of *memory consolidation* into the psychological laboratory. The authors suggested a dual-trace mechanism in which memories are held briefly in the form of a *perseverations-tendenz* (usually translated as reverberation), and later converted into a more permanent structural form if the reverberation is not interrupted. Whether Müller and Pilzecker considered the reverberation to be a sort of neural afterdischarge or something more like a rehearsal process is not certain.

Earlier, Ribot (1892) had postulated that a period of undisturbed neural reorganization was needed to fix memory traces. He based this conclusion on case histories of patients who had suffered memory loss after a head injury severe enough to cause loss of consciousness. These patients usually suffer permanent amnesia for events occurring shortly before the injury, and transient amnesia for still earlier events.

This memory impairment is known as retrograde amnesia. As Polster, Nadel, and Schacter (1991) pointed out in their authoritative review, Müller and Pilzecker's (1900) work was followed by a number of articles relating it to retrograde amnesia and discussing the psychological implications of consolidation. After about 1915, however, little more was heard of consolidation for many years, probably because memory as a legitimate subject for psychological research suffered an eclipse during the era of radical behaviorism in America. Neurologists, however, continued to study amnesic patients (Russell & Nathan, 1946), and the renewed interest in consolidation, when it came, was the result of attempts to learn more about retrograde amnesia.

RETROGRADE AMNESIA

People who have been rendered unconscious by a severe blow on the head or a stroke are very confused immediately after regaining consciousness, and may remember little about their past life. As the confusion clears they often are left with gaps in their memory for recent events and, although in the course of a few weeks most of the memories return, the victims may never remember what happened during the last few seconds or minutes before the accident.

Russell and Nathan (1946) investigated 1000 cases of head injury and found that about 85% of the patients sustained permanent amnesia, the majority for only the few minutes before the injury. In some of these cases, memories from the period of "permanent" retrograde amnesia were recovered under barbiturate hypnosis. Williams and Zangwill (1952) described cases of retrograde amnesia in which more thorough examination revealed unusually poor memory for events that had occurred several days, sometimes even several weeks, before the last (often vivid) memory of the period before injury.

For example, on the day after his accident, one patient had a clear memory of rounding a corner on his bicycle, seeing a bus stopped in front of him, hitting the curb and going over the handlebars. Yet even 3 days later he was still unable to remember that during the week before the accident he had been moved to a different job. Three weeks later, his memory for many events during the week before the accident was still much worse than for similar events in earlier weeks.

Williams and Zangwill (1952) pointed out that prompting or returning to a place where an event occurred sometimes brings a memory back. They considered it likely

> that there are two separate aspects of memory disturbances following head injury: (1) the short and usually complete retrograde amnesia; and (2) more diffuse and widely distributed disturbances of memory for pre-traumatic events. (p. 57).

The first aspect these investigators regarded as a failure to register the input, the second as an impairment of recall.

It probably is significant that the patients remembered very frightening situations that occurred shortly before they lost consciousness, at the same time forgetting earlier, less arousing events. This circumstance suggests that the degree of interference with recall is related to the initial strength of the memory, which in turn depends on the level of arousal associated with the remembered event.

Some confusion concerning the time course of consolidation has never been clearly resolved. The effect of consolidation on recall of word lists, as in Müller and Pilzecker's (1900) experiments, may be observed after a few minutes or hours. Concussion commonly produces permanent amnesia for events that occurred during the preceding few seconds or minutes, but there may be transient amnesia that extends back for several years. It is not very likely that a single process is responsible for all these effects. Certainly, reverberation cannot be expected to retain a memory for as long as a year.

Current research (Bear, 1997; Frey & Morris, 1997, 1998) suggests that arousal modulates the degree to which immediate early genes express a protein needed to increase the long-term effectiveness of recently active synapses. Proteins at synapses exposed to transmitter substance undergo modifications that may last several hours. The change is prolonged greatly by the action of the freshly synthesized protein. If the synapse is disturbed before it can be "fixed" in this way, or if the transcription of the gene is interrupted, the memory is lost.

ELECTROCONVULSIVE SEIZURES

The use of seizures induced by electroshock as a therapy for certain psychiatric disorders, and the discovery soon after its introduction that the treatment led to retrograde amnesias similar to those produced by concussion, opened up the possibility of performing controlled experiments without inflicting serious injury on the subjects (human or other species). Zubin and Barrera (1941) gave patients lists of paired associates to learn just before electroconvulsive treatment and tested recall a few hours later.

When lists were learned on days without electroconvulsive therapy (ECT), there were significant savings on retesting, but none on the days when ECT was given. A disturbance of memory for events during the preceding weeks or months also was observed, but no objective measures of the loss or its rate of recovery were made at that time.

A few years later it was discovered that electroconvulsive shock interfered with learning in animals, triggering a flurry of consolidation experiments on rats, mice, and the occasional chicken. Duncan (1949) performed the first experiment designed to measure the rate of consolidation in animals. He gave different groups of rats electroconvulsive shocks (ECS) at various intervals after each trial in a maze. Learning was impaired in groups that received ECS within a minute or two after the end of each trial, but not when the ECS was longer delayed.

Subsequent research in this area usually employed a one-trial avoidance learning procedure so the time between the trial and the ECS could be controlled more accurately. However, other not-so-carefully controlled conditions apparently are important also. Different experiments yielded consolidation times ranging from a few seconds to many hours.

More recently, the pendulum has swung back toward the use of human subjects. Squire and Cohen (1979, 1982) and Squire, Slater, and Chace (1975) devised tests that provide a more objective measure of the effect ECT has on a patient's remote memories than that obtained by simple questioning. In one experiment, patients were required to identify the names or salient details of television shows from the preceding 16 years that had appeared for one season only. Two versions of the test were administered, one before ECT and the other an hour after a series of five ECT sessions. A control group of patients not undergoing ECT also was tested.

ECT impaired the identification of programs broadcast during the 3 years immediately before the test, but for earlier years the patients achieved scores as high or higher than those of the control group. Some animal studies suggest that the extent of retrograde amnesia is a function of the intensity of the current used to produce seizures (Lee-Teng, 1969). The 3-year limit found by Squire therefore may be a function of the ECT parameters established for optimum therapeutic efficacy, but the result leaves no doubt that memories remain in a vulnerable state for a very long time, far too long for the trace to be retained in a continuously active form. Of course this does not mean that the trace never passes through brief periods of activity.

ANTEROGRADE AMNESIA

The study of retrograde amnesia and consolidation has told us something about the time course of learning, but scrambling the brain with a strong blow or electric current tells us little about the brain structures important for memory. Moreover, retrograde amnesia does not correspond to what is usually called a poor memory. Some people who suffer from a poor memory have relatively well-preserved memories of the past but find it difficult to remember day-to-day events. This is an impairment known as *anterograde amnesia.*

In 1889 Korsakoff reported the case of an alcoholic patient with severe memory loss. In addition to retrograde amnesia (impaired memory for events that happened during the preceding few years), the patient's memory for current events lasted for no more than a few minutes.

This type of amnesia, a fairly common consequence of prolonged excessive alcohol consumption, is a prominent feature of the condition now known as Korsakoff's syndrome. Autopsies have revealed atrophy of many subcortical structures, most frequently parts of the medial thalamus and the mammillary bodies (Adams, Collins, & Victor, 1962; Victor, Adams, & Collins, 1989).

Anterograde amnesia is also an early symptom of Alzheimer's disease, a devastating progressive degenerative disease of the brain that eventually undermines all cognitive processes. Because of its progressive nature, patients with Alzheimer's disease are not very satisfactory subjects for research into memory mechanisms.

Williams and Pennybacker (1954) found that tumors bordering the third ventricle often are accompanied by memory impairment, and several more recently studied cases, to be described, appear to show that lesions confined to the thalamus can result in anterograde amnesia (Gentilini, de Renzi, & Crisi, 1987; Graff-Radford, Tranel, Van Hoesen, & Brandt, 1990; Winocur, Oxbury, Roberts, Agnetti, & Davis, 1984).

Some types of epileptic seizure are known to leave the patient with confusion and amnesia similar to that resulting from ECT or concussion. People in this state sometimes suffer from transient anterograde amnesia, performing long and complicated (but familiar) acts such as setting a dinner table, or driving home from work, and shortly afterward having not the faintest recollection of having done so. Transient global amnesia also can occur in the absence of seizure activity (Strupp et al., 1998), probably as a result of cortical spreading depression (Leão, 1944).

Electroencephalograms show that seizures producing amnesia usually have their focus in the temporal lobe (Gloor, 1960; Penfield & Jasper, 1954). Brown and Schäfer's (1888) and later Klüver and Bucy's (1938) observation of the deficient memory of monkeys with bilateral temporal lobectomy points to the same region. Penfield believed memory to be localized in the temporal cortex because stimulation of that area, in conscious human patients during brain operations, occasionally elicits reports of vivid auditory and visual experiences, described by the patients as reenactments of past events (Gloor, Olivier, Quesney, Andermann, & Horowitz, 1982; Penfield & Perot, 1963).

It has been suggested that this phenomenon is related more closely to dreams and hallucinations than to memories (Squire, 1987), and this seems likely. Nevertheless there is a component of memory in dreams, and it is interesting that although Penfield at one time or another stimulated almost every part of the human cortex, vivid "memories" were aroused only from the temporal lobes.

Stimulation with electrodes that penetrate below the neocortex of the temporal lobe into the vicinity of the hippocampus and amygdala often produce effects on memory that more closely resemble those of concussion or electroconvulsive therapy (Bickford, Mulder, Dodge, Svien, & Rome, 1958; Chapman, Walter, Markham, Rand, & Crandall, 1967; Feindel, 1961; Pampiglione & Falconer, 1960). For a few hours after stimulation the patient may be unable to recall events that took place during the preceding week or two, the extent of the amnesia depending on the intensity and duration of the stimulation. There often is permanent amnesia for the period of the stimulation, and sometimes for a few seconds to a few minutes after it.

MEDIAL TEMPORAL- LOBE INJURY

More direct evidence for the localization of memory mechanisms was provided by the discovery that damage to the medial temporal lobe in humans leads to profound and permanent anterograde amnesia (Penfield & Milner, 1958; Scoville & Milner, 1957). There had been previous reports of memory loss after bilateral lesions of the hippocampal region (Bekhterev, 1900; Glees & Griffeth, 1952), but they provided little information about the nature of the memory impairment.

The most thoroughly studied patient is known by his initials, H.M. In 1953 the medial parts of both his temporal lobes were removed by Dr. William Scoville to alleviate increasingly incapacitating epileptic attacks. After the operation, H.M. had a severe memory impairment that has shown little or no improvement over the years. Recent magnetic resonance images of his brain show that the medial temporal- lobe lesions are not as large as reported by the surgeon (Corkin, Amaral, González, Johnson, & Hyman, 1997). The posterior half of each hippocampus was spared, as were parts of the neighboring cortex. Some atrophy of the cerebellum was found, probably an effect of heavy doses of anti-seizure medication administered during the years before surgery, but it was not considered likely that this atrophy contributed to the amnesia.

Subsequent testing of patients with less widespread bilateral destruction provides strong evidence that damage to the hippocampus proper *(cornu Ammonis)* is sufficient to produce a memory deficit (Milner, Corkin, & Teuber, 1968, p. 231; Zola-Morgan, Squire, & Amaral, 1986), though the impairment is a good deal less severe than that produced by lesions that include adjacent neocortex. More recent research on monkeys suggests that a lesion of the perirhinal cortex, which relays visual input from the temporal neocortex to the hippocampus, produces a more severe memory impairment than a lesion confined to the hippocampus proper (Zola-Morgan, Squire, Amaral, & Suzuki, 1989).

Memory impairment is not difficult to detect in patients with severe anterograde amnesia caused by medial temporal-lobe injury. Although the patients have no difficulty recognizing people they knew for several years before the onset of their amnesia, after their lesion they never learn to recognize nurses and doctors with whom they interact every day. They lose their way in the hospital, forget conversations within a few minutes, and repeatedly ask the same questions. They show little or no improvement with time.

The symptoms are all the more striking because the patients otherwise appear to have normal intelligence. Except for a retrograde amnesia that may extend back over several years, they are said to have no trouble remembering details of their lives before the onset of amnesia (although the generality of this finding has been questioned recently by Nadel and Moscovitch, 1997).

DIENCEPHALIC LESIONS

Similar symptoms of anterograde amnesia have been reported in patients with partial lesions of the diencephalon. Korsakoff patients often have conspicuous lesions of the mamillary bodies, but Adams et al. (1962) found that lesions of the medial thalamic nuclei correlate more closely with amnesia. Several investigators claim to have found severe cases of diencephalic amnesia with no thalamic involvement, including the case of a patient who discovered a shortcut to Korsakoff-like amnesia requiring no more than a single bout of excessive alcohol consumption. In a drunken brawl he was struck by a snooker cue, which passed through his left nostril and penetrated the base of his skull, damaging his pituitary and mamillary bodies (Dusoir, Kapur, Byrnes, McKinstry, & Hoare, 1990). According to magnetic resonance imaging, his thalamus is intact. His amnesia is attributed to a lesion of the hypothalamus.

In the rat (Gaffan, 1972; Packard, Hirsh & White, 1989), and even in the monkey (Gaffan, 1974), cutting the fornix is considered equivalent to partial ablation of the hippocampus by some. Usually the effect is attributed to loss of the afferent adrenergic and cholinergic connections that run through the fornix. Such pathways often show some recovery after a time, due to the sprouting of new terminals and increased receptor sensitivity.

SPARED MEMORY IN AMNESIC PATIENTS

At first it was thought that the anterograde amnesia of H.M. and others with similar lesions was all-embracing or "global." The patients cannot recall events that they have recently seen, heard, or read about. They do not remember their own activities or thoughts. They become lost instantly, except in places familiar to them before their lesion, and they cannot learn maze problems (Milner et al., 1968). Soon, however, it was discovered that these patients acquire and retain motor skills, such as drawing while viewing their work in a mirror, as readily as normal subjects, though the more severe cases deny having any memory of the training sessions (Milner, 1962).

Later, Cohen and Squire (1980) showed that amnesic patients could retain a mirror-reading skill, test instructions, and problem-solving techniques. The patients also remember that they have a memory problem, and recall the strategies used to deal with it. One patient learned to play a tune (South American Way) on the piano after becoming amnesic, and although he never remembered having learned it, he could play it after being given the first few notes (Starr & Phillips, 1970).

Amnesic patients show no loss of. immediate memory span, as measured by their ability to recite a short sentence or a string of digits they have just heard (Penfield & Milner, 1958). If not distracted, H.M. can retain a number for at least 15 minutes by continuously rehearsing either the number or various mnemonics for it (Milner, 1959).

Immediate memory may be attributed to the short-term sequence store (Warrington & Shallice, 1969) described in chapter 5, in which the contents decay below threshold in a few seconds if not refreshed, and are irretrievably overwritten if the attempt is made to store more than about seven items. The impairment appears to be unrelated to the limbic anterograde amnesia syndrome.   Thus, skills and immediate memory are quite unaffected by lesions that severely impair recall and recognition of recent events. Many observations, moreover, indicate that amnesiacs store a great deal of information that is not immediately accessible to their conscious memory (Moscovitch, Goshen-Gottstein, & Vriezen, 1994).

If they are allowed time to study a set of pictures thoroughly, amnesic patients can recognize a significant number of them even after several weeks. Warrington and Weiskrantz (1968) found that a group of amnesic patients improved almost as much as normal subjects in their ability to recognize fragmented drawings of common objects (Gollin, 1960), and retained the improvement for 24 hours. B. Milner (1970) confirmed this in H.M., and found that the improvement in recognition, though inferior to that of normal control subjects, persisted for at least 6 months.

If no consolidation takes place or forgetting is complete, the striking improvement in the perception of fragmented figures and words is impossible to explain. Without long-term storage, the fragments would be no more capable of prompting the correct answer (or restricting the choice of answers) on subsequent presentations than they would have been on the first presentation. Clearly learning has taken place, though lacking some feature necessary for conscious recognition.

REPETITION PRIMING

Tulving and Schacter (1990) considered Warrington and Weiskrantz's (1968) results to be related to another form of memory, called repetition priming, that also is spared in amnesic patients.   An early example of this effect was reported by D. L. Scarborough, Cortese, and Scarborough (1977), who found that normal subjects, in a test to distinguish between words and non-words, responded faster to the second presentation of a stimulus than to the first.

The effect of the priming was still present several days later, even though the subjects did not consciously recognize the repeated stimuli. Experiments on normal subjects show that there is little if any priming effect for nonsense words or figures (Tulving & Schacter, 1990), suggesting that some form of neural representation must be acquired before priming occurs.

DISCRIMINATION

After it had been shown that monkeys with medial temporal-lobe lesions as extensive as those of H.M. could learn visual discriminations (Gaffan, 1974; Mishkin, 1982; Orbach, Milner, & Rasmussen, 1960), it was confirmed that H.M. and other amnesic patients could do the same (Gaffan, 1972; Sidman, Stoddard, & Mohr, 1968). Sidman's group found that H.M. could learn to discriminate a circle from an ellipse and retain the ability for at least several minutes longer than he was able to say what he had been doing. Gaffan trained a patient with severe amnesia to discriminate colors, and although the patient disclaimed all knowledge of the test on the next day, she performed the discrimination perfectly.

It is not surprising that for a time the ability to learn and retain visual discriminations escaped notice, because the patients themselves denied remembering any previous experience with the tests. Perhaps the most interesting thing that emerges from many of these findings is the discrepancy between what the patient can recognize as familiar and the stored information that can be revealed by an appropriate method of testing. It also is apparent that longer periods of study can partly compensate for extensive loss of the hippocampus and surrounding neocortex.

These observations complicate the interpretation of animal experiments. Researchers cannot ask a monkey whether an object appears familiar or not. All they can do is determine whether the monkey's response to an object depends on whether it has seen the object before. Hippocampectomized monkeys learn a visual discrimination as readily as normal monkeys, but they have difficulty performing tests of delayed alternation (Orbach et al., 1960), in which they must remember on which side of the apparatus food was last presented and choose the other side.

Tests of delayed matching also are particularly sensitive to bilateral limbic-system lesions (Gaffan, 1974). The matching-to-sample deficit seems analogous to the deficits of human amnesic patients on delayed same/different tests, in which the subjects are presented with a tone, color, or abstract shape and must say whether it is the same or different from a tone, color or shape presented a short time earlier (Prisco, 1963, cited by Milner, 1968).

In summary, lesions in the medial temporal region produce amnesia of the type that has been most influential in shaping our ideas about the mechanisms of memory. Quite similar memory loss is produced by damage to parts of the diencephalon and other structures closely connected to the hippocampus. Although it seems likely that in these cases the amnesia is due to interference with hippocampal function, the question still is open to debate. All that is known for certain is that damage to any part of a system that includes much of the medial temporal lobe and the medial diencephalon is likely to result in anterograde amnesia. It appears that the more extensive the lesion in that system, the more severe the resulting amnesia is likely to be (Squire, Zola-Morgan, & Alvarez, 1994).

Recently, largely on the basis of animal experiments, there have been attempts to differentiate the functions of various parts of the hippocampal region (Eichenbaum, Otto, & Cohen, 1994; Otto, Schottler, Staubli, Eichenbaum, & Lynch, 1991). Although it seems reasonable to speculate that the various structures of the medial temporal lobe serve different functions, attempts to make specific attributions of function may be premature.

It appears that the rest of the brain can do almost everything that the limbic memory system can do except remember routes and put items on hold for more than a few seconds. Amnesic patients and animals have no difficulty with visual perception, for example. If there is no delay, they can compare stimuli or spatial arrangements of objects. Until the picture of exactly what the memory system is contributing becomes clearer, it will be difficult to apportion that contribution among its different anatomical components.

DIFFERENT KINDS OF LEARNING

The potency of a synapse may be changed in many ways, some of them producing very short-term effects, others leaving permanent traces. The effect of a synaptic change also depends on the circuit in which the synapse is located. A brain lesion has different effects on different kinds of learning (McDonald & White, 1993; Milner, 1962; Mishkin, Malamut, & Bachevalier, 1984; Tolman, 1949; White & Carr, 1985).

Some of the short-term changes play an important role in perception, retaining a word, for example, until its ambiguity is resolved by a subsequent phrase. Disturbance of this function would be seen as a failure of perception rather than a deficit of memory or learning. If the task involves matching one stimulus with another, or holding an instruction until it can be applied, a similar loss of short-term plasticity would be seen as an impairment of short-term or working memory.

EPISODIC MEMORY

In animal experiments, learning almost always is tested by observing how reliably the subject repeats responses that have proved successful in the past. When human beings talk about memory, however, they often mean the ability to recall the events of the day or other past experiences. People often reminisce even when their memories are not being tested. It is one of the things humans do to while away the time.

Some learning, such as learning to speak, enters into every aspect of life, though often we remember nothing about the learning process. At the other extreme are individual events remembered for varying lengths of time, including for life.

General knowledge often is termed semantic memory, whereas memory for a specific event is called episodic memory, a terminology made popular by Tulving (1972). The distinction corresponds roughly to the difference between learning and memory in common usage. What is learned remains as knowledge even after we have forgotten how or when it was learned. We *know* our friends and acquaintances but we *remember* someone we met for a short time last year.

According to this terminology, the model of chapter 2 learns. Remembering is only incidental to the process of performing a learned act. For that purpose, the circumstances under which the initial connections were made are not important, although associations with a particular place, and sometimes with a particular time, may be necessary for eliciting the correct response.

Episodic memory, by definition, is acquired in one trial. Animals such as the rat exhibit lasting one-trial learning under the influence of intense reinforcement such as an electric shock. Stimuli present at the time of reinforcement presumably acquire associations with the emotional effects of the reinforcer, and the learning can later be demonstrated by presenting the same stimuli again, just as for multi-trial learning. Whether an animal ever frightens itself in the middle of the night with memories of the episode, as a person probably would, is difficult to determine.

The more usual method of testing episodic memory in animals is to introduce a delay into a discrimination test. In the classical delayed-response test the animal sees where food is hidden and is allowed to look for it after a delay, usually just a few minutes. In the wild, however, some animals that hide food themselves can find it again months later. The radial maze is a laboratory version of the spatial memory task in which animals must remember the places from which they removed food rather than where they hid it. Again, the delay intervals are short, though under certain circumstances rats interrupted halfway through the task can remember from one day to the next which goal boxes they have not yet visited (Packard & White, 1989).

In all these tasks, it is clear that associations are being established between the neural activities produced by reinforcers and the various times, places, and actions that accompanied them, associations that produce conspicuous changes in subsequent behavior when similar conditions are encountered. Many animals explore their territory until they are familiar with it, even if no conventional reinforcement is there, but it is not easy to discover whether they remember the territory when they are away from it. Do monkeys in the zoo ever reminisce about their days in the jungle? If so, do they have any concept of how long ago those days were? A characteristic of human memories is that they are tagged with the approximate time they were recorded. That information can be used to access a memory, as, for example, when someone answers the question "What did you do this morning?"

The implication of time tagging is that there is a rather elaborate clock calendar in the brain. The clock part may be linked in some manner to the circadian processes that control the rate of synthesis of many hormones. In this way the probability that certain timekeeper neurons acquire associations with perceptual and motor activity could be made to vary with the time of day. Changes during the course of the day in the level of hormones that influence the thresholds of two or three different types of synapse would ensure that events acquire different associations depending on the time of day they occur.

Longer periods could perhaps be estimated by comparing the amounts of residual potentiation at synapses whose potentiations decay at different rates. Thus if the association of an event with a "morning" group of neurons is mainly at synapses whose potentiation decays slowly, with only a weak association remaining at rapidly decaying synapses, the event must have been in the morning some days ago.

Of course, the day-night and summer-winter cycles that gave rise to our biological clocks are still with us, and they have been supplemented by fabricated clocks and calendars. Any or all of these stimuli may provide a time base for memories. As far as I know the problem has not been investigated experimentally. My intention in this discussion is to point out that our ability to remember what we were doing at a particular time, and our ability to say how long ago an event occurred, require events to be associated with brain processes that vary systematically with time. The exact nature of those processes remains to be discovered.

The study of memory for events draws attention to the importance of remembering actions. Asking a friend what she did during they day is likely to elicit a string of verbs: "I got up, washed, ate, 'phoned, walked, shopped, read, dozed, talked, drove, watched television, and so to bed". Neuroscientists who study learning rarely consider the memory for actions. Psychological experiments tend to focus on memory for objects and places, but how information concerning accomplishments is stored also needs to be considered.

SUMMARY

Memory is concerned with time, and in general, scientists are more comfortable with spatial dimensions than with time. This is especially true for behavioral scientists. We can control our progress through space, but whether we like it or not, we are propelled inexorably along the time dimension. Memory is our only means of monitoring this journey, a rearview window to be sure, but better than no window at all. Memory allows us and other animals to use the past to inform our guesses about what the future will bring.

Experience modifies almost everything. Animals have evolved methods of using the changes to their advantage. There are many aftereffects of the reactions that take place at synapses when transmitter substances are released. Some of the effects disappear almost instantly, but others last for varying lengths of time from a few seconds to a lifetime.

Changes that may last for a minute or two are very important for perception. Many stimuli such as words are meaningless in themselves and need to be stored for combining with other stimuli. Characteristics of objects to be compared also need to be stored.

Longer term changes are important for attaching meaning to perceived stimuli. Such meaning is acquired when neurons fired by the stimulus become associated with concurrent activity in the motivation/motor system or other active systems.

Observations of amnesic patients lead to the conclusion that long-term and short-term changes in synaptic effectiveness occur in different regions of the brain. Loss of recent memory after seizures or head injury and the susceptibility of recent learning to interference by later learning indicate that memories require time to become consolidated. The period before a memory is completely consolidated may be several years in humans, though after head injury, usually only events that occurred in the preceding few minutes are permanently forgotten. It has been suggested that brain trauma completely interrupts the recording of a memory, which takes only a short time to complete, and impairs the effectiveness of recently produced synaptic changes for several days or weeks until the damage has healed.

Early theories of consolidation attributed the effect to a two-stage process in which information is first stored as a neural "reverberation," and later by structural changes. Recent evidence suggests that the initial storage involves local modification of receptor and second-messenger proteins, followed some time later by the production of new protein by an effect on gene expression. When undisturbed, the initially affected synapses retain a chemical tag that allows the new protein to find them, and thus produce the more permanent change at the correct synapses.

It is hardly possible that this mechanism can explain the very slow consolidation that protects old memories from the effect of concussion or electroconvulsive shock. It is more likely that intermittent activation over a period of many months strengthens synapses in regions of the brain that are less vulnerable to trauma than the hippocampus and adjacent neocortex.

The evidence that impairment of diencephalic and medial temporal-lobe structures is a major factor in amnesia comes mainly from observing the effects of lesions, but also from brain stimulation, and the localization of seizures that produce amnesia.

A number of suggestions have been made for distinguishing learning that is affected, from learning that is unaffected by lesions of this system, but few of these suggestions cast much light on the neural mechanism of memory. Dysfunction of the mnemonic system impairs habituation, the acquisition of a sense of familiarity, and performances that require rapid storage of new information, as, for example, delayed alternation, delayed matching to sample, rapid extinction of well-established responses, and recall of verbal material longer than the span of immediate memory.

The lesions are less damaging to learning that requires repeated practice such as perceptual learning, some forms of conditioning, and discrimination learning. They completely spare the learning of skills, repetition priming, and the brief storage of items that are within the memory span.

7 Theories of Amnesia

Chapter 6 reviewed observations of the main characteristics of memory storage and its impairment by trauma or lesions of the brain. This chapter deals with some of the neural mechanisms that have been suggested to account for those observations.

FAMILIARITY

The effectiveness of prompting as an aid to recall demonstrates that amnesic patients do store some information. Nevertheless, they do not remember that they have recently seen the pictures or heard the words they can identify. As far as the patients are concerned, their answers are guesswork, correct only by chance. This type of memory is sometimes called implicit because it must be inferred from behavior. The phenomenon is puzzling and invites a closer analysis of what it means to be aware of having experienced an event.

For some authors, Jacoby and Witherspoon (1982), for example, the criterion for memory with awareness is that the subject can give a context to the memory, (who was present, where it occurred, how long ago, etc). But what about the ability merely to say "Yes, I saw that before"? Such an answer would indicate awareness of the prior experience, even if no other episodic content could be recalled. Usually it would be regarded as inconsistent with a diagnosis of anterograde amnesia (Schacter, 1987).

Establishing a criterion for conscious memory would be easier if we understood the mechanism normally involved in recognition. An obvious and frequently offered answer is that recognized stimuli reactivate the same neural circuits they fired when they were first presented. As Mishkin (1982) said in relation to visual recognition: "Recognition occurs when this central representation is reactivated by the same stimulus on a later occasion." (p. 85). And Teyler and DiScenna (1986) said that the partial repetition of an event "can be recognized as a memorial event by its ability to recreate the pattern of neocortical modules activated by the original experiential event" (p. 149).

After due consideration, however, it is seen that this answer does not get to the crux of the matter. The fact that a stimulus is recognized demonstrates that it is activating a neural pattern different in at least one respect from the pattern previously activated. The first time it was perceived, the nervous system categorized it as "novel." When recognized, it loses that label and gets the label "familiar." How are these labels acquired?

Familiarity must be represented by a neural activity, an adjectival engram if you like, that modifies or qualifies substantive engrams. The neural activity resembles those corresponding to such concepts as "small" or "blue" that can modify the meanings of many other concepts. People can select blue objects from a group of colored objects. In like manner, they can select familiar objects (Milner, 1989).

In principle, it is known what blueness involves. Certain neurons in the visual system are fired selectively by short-wavelength light falling on the retina, and if those cells fire at the same time as pattern-recognition neurons are firing in response to the same light, the pattern is perceived as blue. Presumably there are neurons whose firing endows any accompanying pattern-recognition activity with "familiarity." How is this hypothetical familiarity engram, established and how is it activated?

"Blueness" and "smallness" engrams are fired by physical properties of external objects, but whether the familiarity system fires depends only on some condition *within* the nervous system. The same object may be recognized by one observer, and not recognized by another. The first time an object is presented it does not fire the familiarity engram (or if it does so by accident, it is diagnosed as a *déjà vu* experience). Instead, it probably will arouse fear or initiate an investigatory response - reflexive or instinctive reactions common to most vertebrates.

After a few minutes, attention to the new object tapers off as habituation occurs. On subsequent encounters, habituation occurs more rapidly until eventually the object no longer arouses investigation. It appears that repeated experience with a stimulus strengthens a path for suppressing built-in fear and curiosity behavior (see the Habituation section in chapter 9). The system that inhibits investigatory responses has the characteristics required of a familiarity system. I have suggested that the activity of this system, projected to the neocortex and other brain areas, establishes a pattern that constitutes the concept of familiarity, acquiring associations with response circuits needed to pronounce the word "familiar," for example (Milner, 1989).

Subsequently, this neural activity is always present at about the same time as the neural representation of the familiar object. Therefore the "familiarity" engram and the engram of the object that is becoming familiar both acquire associations with the same motivational and motor activity present at the time. Henceforth, whenever the object is perceived the activity it induces in the motor system is transferred to the familiarity engram. This association is at first mainly via the readily modified synapses of the limbic mnemonic circuits, but eventually more permanent connections are forged via neocortical paths. Once that has occurred, the animal no longer needs the limbic connections to associate the object with familiarity, thus objects remain familiar even after removal of the medial temporal lobe.

Rapidity of habituation to benign stimuli is advantageous in the competition for survival, which may account for the importance of the limbic memory circuit, with its more labile synapses, in detecting familiarity. The role of the limbic system in this mechanism is probably twofold. First, it opens a path between sensory input and the system that inhibits responses to novelty. Then when a cortical pattern representing familiarity has been established, the circuit serves its usual function of making temporary associations between concepts, in this case linking the engram of the new object with the engram of familiarity.

After damage to the mnemonic circuit, if insufficient time has elapsed for permanent associations via neocortical paths to be established, the object will lose its familiarity. Furthermore, no recovery is possible because the habituation path that provided the familiarity information no longer functions effectively. From that time on, only stimuli that already have acquired adequate associations with the cortical familiarity system can fire it. The effect can be compared to selective elimination of blue input to the visual system after the concept of "blue" has been established in the rest of the brain. The patient can still remember the sky as being blue, but can never associate blueness with your new coat.

It is worth emphasizing in connection with this account of familiarity that the same pattern of neural activity announces the familiarity of all percepts that possess that property - breakfast cereal, the voice of the news reader on the radio, or whatever. If recognition of the cereal as having been seen before depended only on reactivation of a cereal engram and if recognition of the announcer's voice as having been heard before depended only on the reactivation of a voice engram, then the proverbial little man (or a less proverbial little woman) snooping around in the brain would be needed to detect the common feature - that all are familiar - so that he or she could convey that information to an inquisitive psychologist.

Moscovitch (1995) advanced a somewhat similar theory to explain the consciousness that distinguishes explicit from implicit memory. Consciousness is assumed to result from neural activity that accompanies perception and is postulated to be stored in memory in the same way as any other neural code. If the mnemonic system is impaired, the "conscious awareness" activity is not stored, though the stimulus may be. This could explain examples of implicit learning in which, for example, a subject with medial temporal lobe lesions may learn a visual discrimination without being conscious of having done so.

NEURAL THEORIES OF AMNESIA

The influence of behaviorist thinking was still strong when interest in memory was reviving. Many psychologists assumed, for example, that a single system was responsible for all learning. The discovery that patients with bilateral medial temporal lobe lesions could recall information for only a few seconds after it had been perceived led to the belief that the lesion interfered with consolidation. The subsequent discovery that amnesic patients do, in fact, store some information, but in a form inaccessible to conscious memory, came as a surprise.

Warrington and Weiskrantz (1970) suggested, as an alternative to the consolidation impairment theory, that hippocampal damage prevents new memories from supplanting older ones. Later theories postulated two memory systems: one in the hippocampal area that stored consciously accessible memories, and another that stored learned modifications of behavior. Many different names were given to these hypothetical systems, contextual memory and habit, for example (Hirsh, 1974). Despite the manifest limitations of the pavlovian concept of habit, many embraced Hirsh's suggestion that habit is responsible for learning after injury to the hippocampal mnemonic system. Habit learning usually was thought to involve the basal ganglia (Mishkin & Petri, 1984; Packard et al., 1989). It is now generally recognized that learning is not carried out by a special system and that plasticity is a property of almost all neural tissue. It is not at all surprising that lesions of a single structure do not produce a global incapacity to learn (Vanderwolf & Cain, 1994).

Another problem facing those seeking to understand the role of the hippocampal region in memory concerns the location of the stored information. The data clearly show that neither short-term nor long-term memories are stored exclusively in the mnemonic system circuits (i.e., those in which lesions produce anterograde amnesia). Patients with large, bilateral, medial temporal-lobe lesions can retain new information for several seconds, at the very least, and they never lose memories already firmly consolidated before the onset of their amnesia. Thus, although it was recognized that consolidation must involve a change of synaptic connections outside the hippocampal area, it was not clear how the neurons of the hippocampal memory system manage to influence synapses in the parts of the brain where permanent memories are stored.

Mishkin (1982), who has spent a lifetime tracing the visual pathways through the cortex and has offered a good account of how a visual stimulus is represented there, postulated that a fully analyzed visual signal is fed to the hippocampus and from there to the thalamus. From the thalamus, he speculated that the signal goes to cholinergic nuclei of the basal forebrain, generating a non-specific signal that consolidates recent modifications to cortical synapses. According to Mishkin, this consolidation ensures that when the same visual stimulus is presented again, the same cortical neurons are fired.

Apart from the question raised earlier as to why any change is required to ensure that the same stimulus produces the same effect, a major problem with this hypothesis is that it predicts consolidation of the cortical trace in minutes, or at the most hours, when in fact loss of hippocampal function may result in retrograde amnesia going back for months or even years. Moreover, the theory fails to account for the ability of amnesiacs to store information of which they are not consciously aware.

Van Hoesen (1982) proposed a theory of amnesia based on the strong reciprocal connections shown to exist between the hippocampus and areas of neocortex where lesions produce modality-specific learning deficits (Rosene & Van Hoesen, 1977). He suggested that current sensory input, along with relevant stored information from past experience, is transmitted to the entorhinal cortex and hippocampus where it is modulated by affective input arriving via the amygdala. The resulting output, which has been processed in some way by the hippocampus to ensure its permanence, is then returned for storage to the cortical area in which it originated.

Van Hoesen claimed that this theory explains why neocortical lesions give rise to modality-specific agnosias, whereas hippocampal lesions affect learning in all modalities. Some of the criticisms leveled at Mishkin's theory also may apply to this one. It predicts a more rapid consolidation than that actually observed and a more extensive amnesia after a lesion.

R. Miller and Marlin (1984) drew an analogy between permanent memories and books shelved in a library. They carried the analogy further with the proposal that to facilitate retrieval, the locations of permanent memories are stored in the neural equivalent of a card index, using a more easily changed form of memory for the purpose.

Teyler and DiScenna (1986) later suggested that this "card index" is stored in the hippocampal region, and that long-term potentiation, known to be present there, is the more easily changed form of memory required by the theory. According to their hypothesis, a cortical trace is established almost immediately, but the information cannot be retrieved without the hippocampal index, which normally is stored at the same time.

The index analogy is somewhat unfortunate in that it implies the presence of an agent to consult it. However, in Teyler and DiScenna's model the hippocampus continuously monitors the cortical pattern and, if it finds a partial match to an index previously recorded in the hippocampus, the original pattern is recreated in the cortex. Teyler and DiScenna (1986), like Mishkin and Petri (1984), accept this as the criterion for recognition (erroneously in my view, as pointed out earlier). In this model, recall (as distinct from recognition) appears to depend on the reactivation of associations made at the neocortical level, and the role played by the hippocampal index in this process is less clear.

The problem with most theories of amnesia is that they concentrate on the impairments and pay too little attention to the abilities of patients and animals with memory system lesions. Some time must pass to reveal most of the differences between amnesiacs and normal subjects. If H.M. is given a telephone number, he can dial it right away. Only if you distract him or make him wait for a minute or two does his problem show up.

Moreover, H.M. can answer questions and engage in conversation as long as no delays or distractions are imposed. At zero delay, H.M. makes normal same/different judgments in a recognition test. His brain does almost all the things that normal brains do, suggesting that the memory circuit has no special function other than facilitating the rapid long-term storage of information.

Some years before the phenomenon of long-term potentiation had been demonstrated (Bliss & Lømo, 1970), an attempt to explain retrograde amnesia prompted me to postulate that there must be learning synapses with short and long decay times. In a 1959 conference, *Current Trends in Psychological Theory,* I said:

Before leaving the learning part of the network I should explain why I have divided it into two parts C [neocortex] and L [limbic]. The difference between them is that the neurons in C are capable of slowly establishing permanent interconnections after many repetitions of being fired simultaneously. The neurons in L, on the other hand, have a very long period of decay of primary association (several hours perhaps) but do not form permanent connections. (Milner, 1961b), p. 124.

The title of the quoted article was *The Application of Physiology to Learning Theory*, but perhaps it should have been *The Application of Learning Theory to Physiology*. More recently I attempted to explain some phenomena of anterograde amnesia on the basis of a similar assumption (Milner, 1989).

The hypothesis proposed that events are represented in the neocortex and briefly stored there by a rapidly decaying trace. In the hippocampal area they are stored by a longer-lasting synaptic change. At first, the hippocampal system is responsible for storing the event after the neocortical part of the trace decays, but each time the event occurs or the hippocampal part of the trace is reactivated, a small but permanent increment of the neocortical part of the trace takes place. Eventually, the "hard" neocortical trace acquires enough strength to retain the memory without assistance from the less enduring ("soft") hippocampal-area trace. A somewhat similar theory has been suggested by Squire and his colleagues (Alvarez & Squire, 1994; Squire & Zola-Morgan, 1991).

A few changes to the model must be made to take account of the view developed in chapters 3 and 4 that association between cortical representations of concepts is indirect, mediated by a central executive system. When responding is involved, engrams acquire associations with each other via motor plans, or motivation.

Much of the posterior neocortex is devoted to converting patterns of receptor activity into coded representations of the features of incoming stimuli. According to the theory developed in chapter 3, sensory neurons that have become associated with the current intention of the organism are facilitated by attentional activity from the response planning system via learned reciprocal connections.

Immediate memory is explained by the hypothesis that these connections from the response system to neocortical engram neurons employ learning synapses that decay in a few seconds, leaving only a small permanent increment of synaptic strength each time the path is active. By contrast, the soft synaptic connections from the response system to neurons in the hippocampal and entorhinal regions remain effective for a much longer period, hours or days. Thus, if some hours after the first conjunction of a response with a stimulus an animal is moved to repeat whatever it was doing, the engram neurons most likely to be fired by the intention are in the hippocampal region.

The firing of these neurons has a number of effects. If the stimulus they represent was followed originally by reinforcement, the neurons acquire associations with activity aroused in the response planning system by the reinforcement. If, on the other hand, the neurons represent a stimulus of no motivational interest, they acquire no motivational associations, and their activity provides no encouragement to the response being planned, which then may be abandoned. (Nevertheless, the activity in the hippocampal region would suppress the "novelty" response, so the familiarity system would be activated.)

The firing hippocampal-system neurons also facilitate, via innate reciprocal paths, the neurons at earlier levels of sensory input, mostly to those in the neocortex whose original direct associations from the response planning activity decayed shortly after the event. The facilitation revives the faded association and restores it briefly to full strength. This hippocampally assisted firing of neocortical neurons every time the response plan is active, slowly increases the strength of the hard synaptic connections between the response plan and the neocortical engram of the stimulus.

An extensive lesion of the hippocampus and surrounding region, where the soft learning synapses are concentrated, prevents rapid changes of behavior in response to changes in reinforcement or other environmental conditions. The lesion also removes the system that inhibits reactions to novelty, so that the a new engram never has the chance to become associated with the cortical activity that represents familiarity.

Because the soft synapses retain the effects of a single recent event for several days, they exert a disproportionate influence on behavior during that time. After they have been eliminated by a medial temporal-lobe lesion, learned behavior is determined by whatever neocortical associations were previously established. Switching to a new, or less dominant, behavior pattern must involve the modification of hard synapses, a long and difficult process. In some cases, when a dominant neocortical association has no close competitors, modification of behavior (except very briefly) in the absence of soft synapses may be practically impossible.

This could explain, for example, the failure of hippocampectomized rats to learn one response to get food, and a different response in the same environment to obtain water (Hirsh, 1980). It also elucidates much of the other behavior cited by Hirsh to support the view that hippocampal lesions impair contextual learning. The hypothesis also could explain the lack of behavioral flexibility noted by Cohen and Eichenbaum (1993), as well as Warrington and Weiskrantz's (1970) erstwhile belief that amnesia is a retrieval failure, caused by interference from stronger prior associations.

The retrograde amnesia after head injury can be explained if the process underlying change at soft synapses is more susceptible to injury than that at hard synapses. The permanent amnesia for events occurring shortly before a head injury is presumably caused by the momentary arrest or disruption of chemical processes crucial for the maintenance of synaptic change.

Brief interruption of the learning mechanism by a blow or seizure has a minor effect on hard synapses, which are only slightly modified by a single event, even when functioning normally. During transient failure of storage at soft synapses, however, rapid learning would be drastically impaired because normally those synapses are responsible for most of the immediate learning.

A puzzling component of retrograde amnesia is the post-traumatic, usually transient, inability to retrieve memories of events that happened weeks or months before the brain injury, This phenomenon can be explained by impairment of the vulnerable soft synapses, making associations dependent on the incompletely established, though more robust, hard synaptic connections. Well-established associations based on neocortical connections that may have taken years to develop, and that rely only slightly on support from the mnemonic circuit, are little affected by the trauma. Such associations become available almost as soon as consciousness returns after a severe concussion or complete destruction of the hippocampal region.

Less well-established long-term associations may be inadequate for recall after loss of support from soft synaptic activity. This is clear from H.M.'s permanent retrograde amnesia, which extends for many years before his operation (Corkin, 1984). Recall still may be possible in less serious cases with help from some soft synapses that survive the trauma.

Hard synapses that have accrued (by intermittent activation) for only a few weeks, require a lot of help from soft synapses to elicit an association. Even slight damage to mnemonic circuit neurons may suffice to prevent retrieval of such recent memories unless prompts or other priming techniques are used to compensate for the loss.

The anterograde amnesia that follows destruction of regions containing soft synapses is explained by loss of most of the synapses that provide the initial associations between engrams. This means that learning is slow, and switching from one association to another on the basis of brief recently presented information is impossible, as in delayed matching to sample for example. However the fact that some learning is spared after medial temporal lobe removal suggests that there are relatively soft synapses in regions that escape the lesion.

There is speculation, for example, that the learning of motor skills, which is rarely rapid, depends on synaptic changes in the neocortex, striatum, and possibly the cerebellum (McCormick & Thompson, 1984; Mishkin & Petri, 1984; White, 1989), perceptual learning may be accomplished by synaptic change in the inferotemporal neocortex (Mishkin & Appenzeller, 1987). The work of Warrington and Weiskrantz (1970) mentioned earlier shows that although memory system lesions impair the rapid formation of long-term associations, they do not entirely prevent it.

The experiments showing this most clearly involve cues such as initial letters, that help amnesic patients to recall words from a list learned some time earlier. The words to be remembered are sufficiently common to be familiar to the patients before the onset of memory loss. Thus, it can be assumed that a prompt has the effect of priming the plans to pronounce a number of words, including the one to be remembered. The consequent temporary lowering of the word's threshold may be all that is needed, allowing it to be fired by a weak association, perhaps provided by recently acquired connections via neurons outside the area of the lesion. The thresholds of contextual associations are unaffected by the letter prompts, so the patients have no explicit memory of their previous encounter with the list and think they are just finding any word that will fit the cue.

In summary, the proposed model incorporates three main processes for associating concepts: (a) an instantaneous synaptic change, not confined to mnemonic-circuit synapses, that decays after a few seconds if not frequently refreshed by some rehearsal process, (b) a longer lasting increase in synaptic strength, confined mostly to mnemonic-circuit neurons, that occurs almost immediately and may last for hours, or days (long-term potentiation), and (c) a small but very long-lasting increment in the efficacy of synapses outside the mnemonic circuit that accumulates with repetition and may take years to attain full strength.

SUMMARY

The classification of a stimulus as familiar requires an association between activity responsible for habituation and the representation of the stimulus. Only after the association is consolidated firmly at the neocortical level does familiarity survive damage to the hippocampal - diencephalic mnemonic system.

Shortly after an event occurs, it is stored mainly by connections involving neurons in the medial temporal and diencephalic regions, where easily modified "soft" synapses are concentrated. Behaviors such as alternation, or matching samples, that require the dominance of memory for recent events (working memory) over permanent memory, are seriously impaired if the soft synapses are selectively removed or damaged. Learned behavior then is dependent on "hard" synapses, which are much more difficult to modify.

8 The Motivation/Response System

The previous chapters present the view that behavior is initiated and controlled by an executive neural mechanism referred to as the motivation and response planning system. In this chapter it is suggested that the basal ganglia play a major role in this system, and an attempt is made to show how these nuclei cooperate with cortical engrams to promote useful responses and block potentially harmful ones.

For many years the physiological study of motivation was concerned primarily with the investigation of sensors and autonomic mechanisms responsible for maintaining optimum states of the body. Studies were aimed at discovering how dehydration and depletion of the energy store are detected, for example, and how body temperature is regulated in homoiotherms. The automatic regulatory mechanisms are important, and not too difficult to study experimentally, but the hard psychological questions concern the problem of how motivation influences voluntary behavior, especially learned behavior.

Animals explore, searching for things they need (including knowledge). They learn not to touch hot things and where to find water or companionship. Motivation to attack a trespasser can be redirected to an activity like building a wall. These aspects of motivation are important for a satisfactory understanding of behavior.

MOTIVATING STIMULI

Discovering the physiological distinction between stimuli that are innately motivating and those that are purely informative is fundamental to an understanding of motivation. In the model developed in chapter 2, most stimuli cease to provoke fear, arousal, or exploratory behavior after they have become familiar. Some stimuli, however, never cease to be avoided or approached, presumably because they excite innately non-habituating pathways.

Discovering why these pathways do not habituate would go a long way toward explaining what motivation is, and how it works. Motivating stimuli, as their name implies, have a modulatory effect on responding. The motor system should therefore be a good place to start looking for clues to motivation.

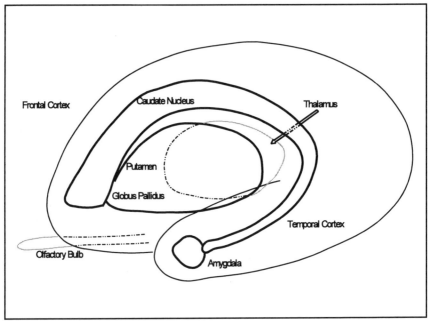

FIG. 8.1.   Basal ganglia.

RESPONSE MODULATION: THE BASAL GANGLIA

At one time most of the nuclei lying below the cerebral cortex were referred to as the basal ganglia, but now the term usually is restricted to the striatum, globus pallidus, subthalamic nuclei, substantia nigra, and some smaller nuclei that also have motor functions (Fig. 8.1). The basal ganglia have long been known to play an important part in responding, and more recently interest has turned to their role in cognition and learning (Alexander & Crutcher, 1990a, 1990b; Everitt, Morris, O'Brien, & Robbins, 1991; McDonald & White, 1993; Milner, 1976: Mishkin, Malamut, & Bachevalier, 1984; Mogenson, Jones, & Yim, 1980; Robbins, Cador, Taylor, & Everitt, 1989; Smith & Bolam, 1990; White, 1989; White & Hiroi, 1998).

As early as 1841, Magendie observed that bilateral destruction of the caudate nucleus (part of the striatum) and adjacent white matter in rabbits made them run irrepressibly forward. A century later, F. A. Mettler and Mettler (1942) reported that after similar lesions, some cats continue to make walking movements even when they are stuck with their head in a corner (*obstinate progression*). In rats, small electrolytic lesions of the caudate-putamen (less than 20%of the nucleus) cause a significant increase in locomotor activity a week after the operation, but the effect subsides 4 to 6 weeks later (Green, Beatty, & Schwartzbaum, 1967).

The head of the caudate nucleus lies immediately below the frontal cortex, from which it receives much of its input.   Bianchi (1895), in the course of investigating the function of the frontal lobes in primates, observed that monkeys with bilateral frontal lobectomy engage in stereotyped pacing and running. Since Bianchi's time, many similar observations have been reported (French & Harlow, 1955; Isaac & De Vito, 1958; Richter & Hines, 1938; Ruch & Shenkin, 1943). Several of these investigators noted that lesions encroaching on the caudate nucleus exacerbated the hyperactivity, leading to speculation that the hyperactivity after frontal lesions might be caused by reduced input to the underlying dorsal striatum.

More recently, it has been shown that the drug MK-801 also increases locomotor activity (Ford, Norman, & Sanberg, 1989). As an antagonist of striatal glutamate receptors that receive cortical input, MK-801 temporarily produces an effect similar to that of a cortical lesion.

The ventral striatum (nucleus accumbens) receives much of its input from the hippocampus and amygdala.   After a temporal lobectomy that destroys these structures bilaterally, monkeys investigate the same object over and over again. Brown and Schäfer (1888) commented on the behavior of a monkey after bilateral temporal lobectomy:

> Every object with which he comes in contact, even those with which he was previously most familiar, appears strange and is investigated with curiosity. And even after having examined an object in this way with the utmost care and deliberation, he will, on again coming across the same object accidentally even a few minutes afterwards, go through exactly the same process, as if he had entirely forgotten his previous experiments. (p. 321).

Similar behavior was noted in temporal lobectomized monkeys 50 years later by Klüver and Bucy (1939).   In rats, hippocampal or fornix lesions cause hyperactivity (Green et al., 1967) or persistent exploratory behavior (Leaton, 1965; Roberts, Dember & Brodwick, 1962; H. Teitelbaum & Milner, 1963). Some of these effects probably result from reduced input to the striatum.

Many motor disabilities are caused by pathologies of the basal ganglia. Involuntary movements such as those of chorea and athetosis result from lesions of the striatum or subthalamic nuclei. In the striatum, the hippocampus, and parts of the neocortex, electrical stimulation has an effect opposite to that of a lesion, inhibiting movement (French, 1959; Kaada, 1951).

Apparently the striatum is part of a system activated by input from parts of the neocortex, hippocampus, amygdala, and thalamus that has a predominantly inhibitory effect on response mechanisms. Such an arrangement might be expected to suppress exploration of stimuli that induce strong activity in the cortex or limbic system. Is there any evidence that rewarding stimuli could antagonize this response inhibition?

DOPAMINERGIC AFFERENTS TO THE BASAL GANGLIA

The medial forebrain bundle contains many pathways, including two major dopamine paths: the nigrostriatal and the mesolimbic. The first originates in the substantia nigra *pars compacta* (SNc) and terminates mainly in the caudate-putamen (dorsal striatum). The second originates in the ventral tegmentum and terminates in several forebrain structures, including the nucleus accumbens (ventral striatum), the olfactory tubercle (also considered part of the ventral striatum), the globus pallidus, and parts of the cortex (Fallon & Loughlin, 1985; Ungerstedt, 1971a).

A number of experiments have shown that stimulation of the input to the striatum from the substantia nigra and tegmental nuclei, has an excitatory or releasing effect on an animal's behavior. Ranson and Magoun (1933) discovered that electrical stimulation of the hypothalamus produces vigorous running movements in cats that are lightly anesthetized and held in a sling. This finding has been replicated a number of times, using cats and other animals (Hinsey, 1940; Rioch & Brenner, 1938; Waller, 1940). The effect is most pronounced when the stimulating electrode is in the lateral hypothalamus which, as we now know, is traversed by the medial forebrain bundle.

Christopher and Butter (1968) elicited what they described as exploratory behavior by continuous electrical stimulation of the lateral hypothalamus in unanesthetized rats.   Under suitable conditions, stimulation of the lateral hypothalamic region may elicit more specific "stimulus-bound" activities such as eating, drinking, sexual behavior, and so on, often interspersed with bouts of running (Beninger, 1983; Ettenberg & Milner, 1977; Gold, Swerdlow, & Koob, 1988; Mattingly, Gotsick, & Salamanca, 1988; Valenstein, Cox, & Kakolewski, 1968). It is tempting to attribute at least a part of these response-potentiating effects of lateral hypothalamic stimulation to the firing of the dopaminergic afferents to the striatum.

Ever since the recognition of dopamine as a brain neurotransmitter (Dahlström & Fuxe, 1964), it has been known that atrophy of neurons in the *pars compacta* of the substantia nigra, the origin of the nigrostriatal path, is associated with Parkinson's disease (Hornykiewicz, 1966), a prominent symptom of which is difficulty in initiating voluntary responses. Similar impairments of responding can be produced by lateral hypothalamic lesions that interrupt the medial forebrain bundle bilaterally, or by a large dose of a neuroleptic, such as haloperidol or pimozide, that blocks the synaptic action of dopamine (Marshall & Teitelbaum, 1977; White, 1986).

On the other hand, amphetamine, a potentiator of dopamine, promotes activity, and in large doses causes persistent repetition of simple movements referred to as stereotyped behavior (Randrup, Munkvad, & Udsen, 1963; Robbins, 1976). A unilateral lesion of the medial forebrain bundle in rats produces circling toward the side of the lesion, the damaged side being partially paralyzed. The animals eventually recover, but the effect of the lesion can be reinstated temporarily by amphetamine, which can release dopamine only from the intact terminals on the side opposite to the lesion (Ungerstedt, 1971b).

Unilateral electrical stimulation of the *pars compacta* of the substantia nigra also causes circling (Vaccarino & Franklin, 1982). These results provide further evidence that striatal dopamine has a facilitatory effect on motor activity. Another finding bearing out the suggestion that response thresholds are linked strongly to the level of dopamine release in the striatum is that amphetamine (or caffeine, which similarly potentiates the effect of dopamine) delays, or even prevents, the extinction of learned responses (Skinner & Heron, 1937).

The involvement of the dopamine paths does not, of course, rule out the possibility that responses are influenced in other ways by the lateral hypothalamus. In fact, data from brain-stimulation reward experiments emphasize the importance of non-dopaminergic pathways.

PHYSIOLOGICAL BASIS OF REWARD

J. Olds and Milner (1954) discovered that rats learn to press a lever, or run a maze, for electrical stimulation delivered to any of a number of sites in the brain. Later, M. E. Olds and Olds (1963) identified the medial forebrain bundle, where it passes through the lateral hypothalamus, as one of the most effective sites for reward. Rats will cross an electrified grid to reach a place where stimulation is delivered. For reviews see Gallistel, Shizgal, and Yeomans (1981), Milner (1991), J. Olds and Olds (1965), J. Olds (1976).

Thus, stimulation of the medial forebrain bundle not only releases such responses as running and exploring, it also establishes the expectation of reward. There are some minor differences between brain-stimulation reward and conventional rewards such as food or water (probably attributable to the absence of any innate appetite for brain-stimulation reward), but the similarities are impressive. There is little reason to reject the hypothesis that conventional rewards and brain-stimulation reward produce their motivating effects in much the same way (Beninger et al., 1987; Ettenberg & Camp, 1986a, 1986b; Wise, Spindler, & Legault, 1978). If such is the case, it may provide clues to the question posed earlier regarding the neural features that characterize rewarding stimuli.

Olds and his colleagues (Olds, Killam & Bach-y-Rita, 1956; Olds & Travis, 1960) also discovered that administering chlorpromazine, a catecholamine antagonist, impairs brain-stimulation reward. This finding has been replicated often using other neuroleptics, some of them specific blockers of dopamine (Ettenberg, 1989; Ettenberg & Duvauchelle, 1988; Fouriezos, Hansson, & Wise, 1978; Fouriezos & Wise, 1976; Mogenson, Takigawa, Robertson, & Wu, 1979; Nakajima, 1986, 1988, 1989; Nakajima & Baker, 1989; Stellar, Kelley, & Corbett, 1983), strengthening the hypothesis that the catecholamine involved in reward is dopamine.

Micro injections of neuroleptic into various parts of the striatum have shown that dopamine's effect on self-stimulation is confined mainly to the nucleus accumbens (Kurumiya & Nakajima, 1988; Mogenson et al., 1979; Mora, Sanguinetti, Rolls, & Shaw, 1975; Stellar & Corbett, 1989). Nevertheless, the precise role of this transmitter in self-stimulation and other rewards has proved elusive (Blackburn, Phillips, Jakubovic, & Fibiger, 1986, 1989; Damsma, Pfaus, Wenkstern, Phillips, & Fibiger, 1992).

The rewarding electric current from the hypothalamic electrode normally does not stimulate medial forebrain bundle dopamine axons directly, although it releases dopamine in the striatum. Measurements of the electrophysiological characteristics of the reward axons stimulated by the electric current show that they are mostly small myelinated fibers, conducting impulses in the rostral to caudal direction (Bielajew &

Shizgal, 1986; Rompré & Shizgal, 1986) whereas the axons of the nigrostriatal and mesolimbic dopamine paths are unmyelinated and normally conduct in the opposite direction.

The explanation usually offered for this paradox by supporters of the dopamine theory of reward is that the stimulated myelinated axons synapse in the midbrain with dopamine neurons, whose ascending axons release dopamine in the striatum and other parts of the forebrain (Bozarth, 1987; Phillips, Blaha, & Fibiger, 1989; Wise & Rompre, 1989). This is a plausible hypothesis (though attempts to demonstrate it have so far proved inconclusive.) In any case, the response of the dopamine system is too sluggish to account for all aspects of self-stimulation behavior (Milner, 1991).

Other evidence for the facilitatory effect of dopamine on reward is that substances like nicotine and heroin, which stimulate dopaminergic neurons in the midbrain, are reinforcing or addictive (Broekkamp, 1976; Rompré & Wise, 1989), as are substances such as amphetamine and cocaine that potentiate the action of dopamine. Of course, these drugs affect many other pathways, so the evidence is not conclusive, but it seems quite well established that dopamine has at least a modulatory effect on reward (Miliaressis, Malette, & Coulombe, 1986; Yim & Mogenson, 1989), and that it helps to counteract the suppression of responding caused by striatal activity (Yim & Mogenson, 1988).

BASAL GANGLIA CONNECTIONS

The neural circuits of the basal ganglia are complicated, and as yet they are by no means fully understood. Because of this, any attempt to explain the effects of lesions and stimulation in terms of the internal connections of the basal ganglia must be somewhat tentative.

Graybiel and Ragsdale (1978, 1983) found that the dorsal striatum (made up of the caudate nucleus and putamen) is divided into two compartments that can be distinguished histochemically. The larger body of the structure (matrix) is richer in acetylcholinesterase than the smaller compartment (striosome), which worms its way around in the matrix. (In an acetylcholinesterase-stained section, the striosome appears as a number of lighter patches, so an alternative name for it is the patch compartment.)

The striosome neurons send a strong projection to the dopamine neurons in the *pars compacta* (SNc) of the substantia nigra, and they receive strong return connections. This suggests that one of striosome's functions may be to regulate the level of dopamine activity in the striatum. The striosome bears a greater functional resemblance to the ventral striatum than to the matrix. White and Hiroi (1998) found, for example, that stimulating electrodes in or adjacent to the striosome are much more likely to support self-stimulation than electrodes in the matrix.

Graybiel (1990) and others (DeLong, Crutcher, & Georgopoulos, 1985; Jiménez-Castellanos & Graybiel, 1989; Parent, 1990) reported that the matrix is further divided into groups of neurons with different histochemical properties and connections. These groups belong to a number of relatively independent but similarly organized parallel systems that, via the globus pallidus, link different cortical (including paleocortical) areas with tectal, pontine, and thalamic motor nuclei (Alexander, DeLong, & Strick, 1986).

The principal neurons of the striatum are of medium size with prominent dendritic spines. Their main neurotransmitter is the inhibitory amino acid, gamma aminobutyric acid (GABA). Most, if not all, of these neurons also contain peptides, which may act as neuromodulators or produce other changes in target cells (Graybiel,

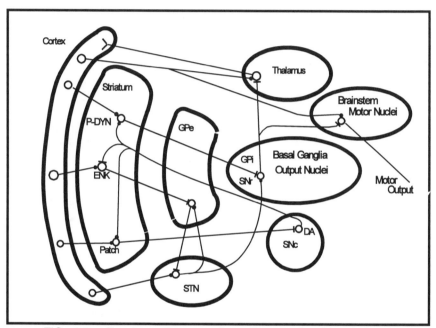

FIG. 8.2.   Basal ganglia connections. (See text for abbreviations.)

1990).

There is a close correlation between the type of peptide a medium spiny neuron secretes and the area to which it projects (Fig. 8.2.). According to Alexander and Crutcher (1990a) and Gerfen (1992) the axons of cells containing substance P and dynorphin (P-DYN) go directly to the internal segment (GPi) of the globus pallidus (entopeduncular nucleus in the rat) and the *pars reticulata* (SNr) of the substantia nigra. These are the output nuclei of the basal ganglia. The axons of cells containing enkephalin (ENK) terminate on neurons in the external segment (GPe) of the globus pallidus, which transfer the signal to the output nuclei via the subthalamic nuclei in a manner to be described shortly.

Globus pallidus neurons are also GABAergic, and the additional inhibitory link in the indirect (ENK) path means that the enkephalin-containing striatal neurons have an effect on the basal ganglia output nuclei opposite to that of the direct path neurons containing substance P and dynorphin.

The principal neurons of the output nuclei are also GABAergic, inhibiting targets in the thalamus and brainstem motor nuclei. As in the cerebellum, the preferred method of signaling in the basal ganglia is by inhibiting (and releasing from inhibition) neurons that have a high background rate of firing. Contributing to this high firing rate is an excitatory input from the cortex which is relayed by glutamatergic neurons of the subthalamic nuclei (STN).

Neurons in the *pars reticulata* of the substantia nigra and both segments of the globus pallidus are fired vigorously via this route, inhibiting brainstem motor nuclei and nuclei of the thalamus. The subthalamic nucleus thus constitutes another relay through which increased cortical activity attenuates responding.

Lesions of the subthalamic nuclei severely attenuate the activity of the internal segment of the globus pallidus and the *pars reticulata* of the substantia nigra, resulting in hyperkinetic motor disorders such as hemiballismus (involuntary flailing of the limbs) as a consequence of the release from inhibition of the thalamus and midbrain motor nuclei. A lesion of the frontal cortex, which cuts off some of the excitatory input to the subthalamic nuclei, produces a similar, but milder, loss of motor inhibition.

If the activity of the indirect (ENK) striatal path is increased, by more input from the cortex for example, the activity of the external segment of the globus pallidus is attenuated. This in turn reduces the inhibition of the subthalamic nuclei, resulting in increased activity of the basal ganglia output nuclei and thus increased inhibition of the motor system. On the other hand, increased activity of the direct path (substance P + dynorphin) inhibits the output nuclei, reducing motor inhibition.

Alexander and Crutcher (1990b) therefore suggested that the indirect path maintains a tonic background inhibition of the motor system, from which the direct path releases selected responses. The direct path does this by suppressing the activity of certain neurons of the basal ganglia output nuclei, thereby releasing a specific motor activity.

An important feature of this dual path through the striatum is that, depending on whether cortical input is delivered to enkephalin-containing neurons or substance P+dynorphin-containing neurons of the striatum, a corresponding part of the response system is either inhibited or released from inhibition.

SYNAPTIC EFFECTS OF DOPAMINE

It has been suspected for some time that dopamine may have either facilitatory or inhibitory effects, depending on the type of receptor to which it binds (Cools & van Rossum, 1980). Several lines of evidence suggest that striosome neurons and direct path (P-DYN) neurons have predominantly D_1 (facilitatory) dopamine receptors, and that indirect path (ENK) neurons have predominantly D_2 (inhibitory) dopamine receptors (Pan, Penny, & Young, 1985; Young, Bonner, & Brann, 1986).

The results of these experiments support the hypothesis that dopamine afferents to medium spiny neurons inhibit those of the indirect path and facilitate those of the direct path (as indicated in Fig. 8.2). As Alexander and Crutcher (1990b) pointed out, the opposing synaptic effect of dopamine on the two types of striatal neurons is offset by the opposing effects of the direct and indirect paths that result from the additional inhibitory link in the indirect path. Thus, dopamine levels determine the relative effectiveness of the two paths (Gerfen, 1992).

Increased dopamine in the striatum has an excitatory effect on the motor system via both direct and indirect medium spiny neuron paths. Neuroleptics, by antagonizing the effect of dopamine, have the opposite effect. They reduce the direct path inhibition of the output nuclei and increase their excitatory bombardment via the indirect path, thereby increasing the inhibition they deliver to motor nuclei.

A lesion of the cortex or striatum removes inhibition from the external segment of the globus pallidus, allowing it to depress subthalamic nuclei activity, which already is reduced by the loss of cortical input. This eliminates most of the excitatory input to the output nuclei, reducing their ability to inhibit motor nuclei. It also reduces the inhibition of the substantia nigra *pars compacta* dopamine neurons, increasing the dopamine input to the striatum.

All these effects reduce the activity of neurons in the output nuclei of the basal ganglia, releasing the response pathways. Although reduced activity of the direct path might be expected to offset this effect by reducing the inhibition of output neurons, removal of inhibition has little effect on neurons deprived of excitatory input.

Almost all cortical areas feed into the striatum. The cortical areas that receive projections, via the thalamus, from the basal ganglia include the prefrontal cortex and the supplemental and premotor areas, in addition to the motor cortex. Thus, motivational input to the basal ganglia influences responding in a very broad sense that can include planning (or "thinking about") responses.

Excessive dopaminergic activity in the striatum, caused either by disease or drugs, is known to produce "forced" pathological thinking. The loss of inhibitory control is somewhat analogous to the loss of motor control in hyperkinetic afflictions such as athetosis or hemiballismus. In the "bad old days," prefrontal lobotomy was performed as a therapy for schizophrenia, but now pathological thinking is controlled by drugs that block excessive dopaminergic activity in the striatum, thus reducing thalamic input to the prefrontal cortex.

SUMMARY

Responding is regulated by motivation, so the response system is a good place to look for behavioral effects of motivation. It has long been known that the striatum (caudate, putamen, and nucleus accumbens) influences response vigor. Animals with large lesions of the striatum become hyperactive. Stimulation of the structure inhibits movement.

The main excitatory input to the dorsal striatum is the frontal cortex, where lesions also produce hyperactivity. The tail of the caudate receives input from a large region of the posterior neocortex. The ventral striatum (nucleus accumbens) receives input mainly from the hippocampus and amygdala, and hippocampal lesions in animals are known to prolong exploratory behavior. This suggests that the striatum is at least partly responsible for the decline in activity during habituation.

The basal ganglia receive additional input from the substantia nigra and nuclei in the ventral tegmentum via the medial forebrain bundle. Stimulation of this pathway as it passes through the hypothalamus invigorates the animal, often releasing some innately organized activity such as running or eating. Medial forebrain bundle stimulation increases dopamine level in the striatum.

Degeneration of midbrain dopamine nuclei is a cause of Parkinson's disease, an affliction in which the patient has difficulty initiating voluntary movements. A similar deficit is produced in animals by lesions of the medial forebrain bundle. Many experiments indicate that dopamine has an important modulatory effect on the activity of striatal neurons.

Animals learn to deliver medial forebrain bundle stimulation to themselves, indicating that it is rewarding. Probably the dopamine released in the striatum during reward serves to facilitate innate responses to rewarding stimuli. Drugs such as amphetamine and caffeine that enhance the effect of dopamine also lower response thresholds. The fact that dopamine antagonists (neuroleptics), administered either systemically or directly to the ventral striatum, attenuate self-stimulation also indicates that dopamine plays a role in reward.

Nevertheless, it is clear that dopamine is not solely responsible for reward. Medial forebrain bundle reward depends mainly on the electrical stimulation of small myelinated axons, but dopamine fibers are unmyelinated. It is possible that cortical input to the striatum acquires rewarding properties by association when it arrives there at the same time as an increase in striatal dopamine.

The principal neurons of the striatum are GABAergic. Most also contain various peptides, including dynorphin, substance P, and enkephalin. Neurons of the basal ganglia output nuclei (internal globus pallidus, or entopeduncular nucleus, and substantia nigra *pars reticulata)* also are GABAergic and inhibit thalamic and midbrain motor nuclei. Striatal neurons containing substance P and dynorphin go directly to the output nuclei, inhibiting the neurons there and thus releasing motor nuclei from inhibition. Striatal neurons containing enkephalin (the indirect path) go to the external pallidum, inhibiting neurons that normally inhibit the subthalamic nuclei. Indirect path activity therefore results in increased excitation of the output nuclei and increased motor inhibition.

Thus the direct path (P-DYN) disinhibits motor nuclei, and the indirect path (ENK) inhibits them. Both paths receive excitatory input from the cortex, but they have different dopamine receptors. The direct path has D_1 (facilitatory) and the indirect path has D_2 (inhibitory) receptors.

Dopamine therefore acts as a switch, turning on the path that disinhibits motor nuclei and turning off the path that inhibits them. Both of these actions lower motor thresholds. Thus, dopamine and its agonists promote behavioral activity and neuroleptics depress it.

9 Basal Ganglia: Behavioral Functions

Chapter 8 presented the argument that the basal ganglia have an important influence on the intensity of motor output. The basal ganglia, in conjunction with the thalamus and cortex, also play an important role in the elaboration and selection of responses a role corresponding roughly to the motivation and response generator complex of Fig. 2.2. The possible contributions of the basal ganglia to a variety of learning situations are outlined in this chapter.

HABITUATION OF FEAR AND CURIOSITY

As mentioned in chapter 2, habituation is an almost universal form of learning. For obvious reasons, most animals have an innate wariness of unfamiliar stimuli, but if this behavior were to persist indefinitely it would seriously dislocate their lives. Fortunately, if the stimulus proves to be inoffensive the cautious behavior wanes. After a period during which an unfamiliar stimulus is avoided, animals usually start to investigate it, another useful innate tendency. In time, this activity also subsides. One of the basic benefits conferred by learning is that these time- and energy-consuming precautions need not be repeated every time the stimulus is encountered.

A neural mechanism that may explain the initial alarm caused by a novel situation is illustrated in Fig. 9.1. Sensory neurons that have never before been strongly excited are fired, activating an arousal/alarm system. The alarm system drives several neural circuits to evoke the behaviors usually associated with fear: startle, freezing, high muscle tone, increased vigilance, adrenalin release with its attendant heart-rate, vascular and intestinal changes, and so forth.

Monkeys with amygdala lesions exhibit a greatly reduced fear response and usually are unaggressive (Klüver & Bucy, 1939; Rosvold, Mirsky, & Pribram, 1954), which suggests that at least some aspects of the alarm response involve the amygdala. The central nucleus of the amygdala has important autonomic efferents, accounting for cardiac, vascular, and hormonal components. Somatic responses to fear (freezing, inhibition of non-reflexive responses, high muscle tone) may involve the basal ganglia, which receive input from the basolateral nucleus of the amygdala. It is probably significant that an attempt to condition the (autonomic) galvanic skin response (GSR) in HM, the patient with a bilateral medial temporal-lobe lesion (which includes the amygdala), was unsuccessful because he showed no GSR response (Kimura, cited by B. Milner et al., 1968).

The mollusk *Aplysia* has a simple mechanism for adapting to novel stimuli. In that animal, synapses between the sensory input and defensive reflexes undergo long-term depression (LTD) with use (Castellucci & Kandel, 1974). A similar mechanism may be at work in the habituation of higher animals. However, lesions of the pedunculopontine tegmental nucleus in rats can impair adaptation to mazes or social situations (Leri & Franklin, 1996; Podhorna & Franklin, 1998), and septal area lesions impair adaptation of startle responses and attack, even in response to gentle

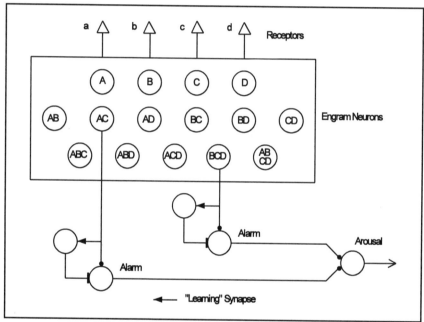

FIG. 9.1.   Habituation to fear of novel stimuli.

and innocuous stimuli (Brady & Nauta, 1953). It therefore seems likely that in mammals, habituation involves learning in specialized inhibitory pathways, as indicated in Fig. 9.1.

The perceptual system depicted is quite unrealistic, but it illustrates how any novel combination of sensory inputs can stimulate previously unfired neurons connected to the alarm mechanisms. In the absence of aversive stimulation, inhibitory paths are activated via learning synapses and eventually attenuate the fear.

Animals also are attracted by unfamiliar objects. Once they have overcome their fear, they approach and carefully examine any strange object. Even after they have just received an electric shock and are still afraid, rats scrutinize the source of the shock from a safe distance (Hudson, 1950). Clearly, it is important to learn as much as possible about a new stimulus, especially if it should be avoided. The suggestion in chapter 2 that lack of information promotes exploration by lowering response thresholds may be realized by the basal ganglia.

Inability to predict the outcome of a planned response could reduce engram activity in the cortex, depriving the striatum and subthalamic nuclei of some input, a state of affairs long known to reduce motor thresholds and produce hyperactivity. This might explain the release of the response plans, whatever they were, enabling their consequences to be experienced and remembered.

As discussed earlier, release of the response system from inhibition is a characteristic of reward, so it may be said that unfamiliar stimuli have a rewarding component. It is even possible to become addicted to novelty and uncertainty, which may explain why tourism and gambling are both multi billion-dollar industries. Most stimuli become less attractive, however, as they become familiar and predictable.

A possible reason for the impoverished cortical (including hippocampal) input to the striatum in an unfamiliar but not unduly stressful situation, is that rarely used synapses of those paths are relatively ineffective. Glutamatergic synapses of the cortico-striate pathways employ n-methyl-d-aspartate (NMDA) receptors, which are found in many pathways where learning occurs. Such synapses become much more effective after having been subjected to strong bursts of afferent impulses.

A weak response of the subthalamic nucleus when an unfamiliar object is under scrutiny means that the excitatory input to the output nuclei of the basal ganglia is reduced. Subthalamic nucleus activity is further reduced by inhibition from the external globus pallidus, which fires more vigorously because weak cortical input to the indirect striatal path reduces the amount of inhibition delivered to it.

Furthermore, low cortical input to the patch neurons reduces the inhibition of midbrain dopamine cells, which may be responsible for at least some of the increased striatal dopamine observed during unfamiliar stimulation. The increased dopamine facilitates the direct striatal path, which further reduces the inhibition of motor nuclei. Avoidance, approach, and other innate responses to sensory stimulation may thus be elicited with little restraint from the basal ganglia.

During the episodes of intensified motor activity, however, repeated encounters with a novel stimulus potentiate synapses from the neocortex, hippocampus, and amygdala to the striatum, and from the cortex to the subthalamic nucleus. A further decline in response vigor results because if the novel input is not reinforcing in any way, increased cortical input to patch neurons in the striatum tends to inhibit midbrain dopamine neurons. These changes allow the striatum to revert to its role of inhibiting the response system, and the investigatory behavior diminishes and stops.

At first, this habituation depends on short-term changes in limbic synapses, so the behavior may start again after a few minutes. However, with repeated exposure over a period of days or weeks, long-term synaptic changes develop, and the stimulus, no longer novel, consistently fails to elicit a response.

REINFORCERS

The rewarding effect of experiencing new things diminishes as the novelty wears off, but loss of response due to habituation must, of course, be reversible in case the stimulus should later become important for the well-being of the animal. Nor should habituation occur in the first place if the stimulus is innately punishing or rewarding.

If a stimulus is punishing, it usually elicits defensive reflexes at a spinal or brainstem level, at the same time inhibiting ongoing centrally generated responses, which were probably what got the animal into trouble in the first place. In higher animals, punishing stimuli gain access to the striatum through various nuclei of the amygdala and thalamus (White & Milner, 1992).

Rewards can prevent or dispel habituation in several ways. They are almost always arousing, thereby increasing the release of dopamine in the basal ganglia. They innately evoke specific approach and consummatory responses (Glickman & Schiff, 1967), a process that presumably involves releasing the responses from basal ganglia inhibition.

Increased release of dopamine in the striatum changes the way medium spiny neurons respond to cortical input. Dopaminergic afferents to the striatum are known to terminate on the more distal dendritic spines of the neurons. In many cases the dopamine terminals occupy the same spines as terminals from cortical afferents (Smith & Bolam, 1990), ensuring that they have a maximum influence on the cortical input.

According to the evidence cited in chapter 8, medium spiny neurons of the direct path (P-DYN) have excitatory dopamine synapses. Their thresholds are therefore reduced by increased dopamine release during reward, ensuring that they are fired more vigorously by cortical input. Increased dopamine at direct path synapses may also promote synaptic change, producing a long-lasting increase in the effectiveness of concurrent cortical input. The resulting increased responsiveness of direct path neurons tends to disinhibit motor nuclei by inhibiting neurons of the output nuclei of the basal ganglia (substantia nigra *pars reticulata* and internal globus pallidus).

The indirect path neurons (ENK) have inhibitory dopamine synapses, so the effect of dopamine on those neurons also should dishabituate the behavior. By enabling the direct path neurons and disabling those of the indirect path, increased dopamine releases any behaviors being generated by the central motor apparatus at the time. In naive animals, the responses released would be those innately evoked by environmental stimuli, hence the stereotyped exploratory behavior produced by large doses of amphetamine.

The general lowering of response threshold by dopamine release also may account for the variable effects of electrical stimulation of the lateral hypothalamus. Valenstein et al. (1968) found that in undeprived rats, the behavior elicited by hypothalamic stimulation often depends on what objects are present, eating when food is present, for example, or drinking when water is present. When no rewarding object is present, the stimulation produces other high-probability behaviors such as sniffing and searching, similar to the stereotyped behavior produced by amphetamine.

The failure of animals to extinguish a learned response under the influence of a dopamine agonist (Skinner & Heron, 1937) also suggests that increased striatal dopamine releases or potentiates responses, learned or innate, most likely to be evoked under the circumstances.

Release of dopamine in the striatum is spatially and temporally diffuse. Presumably, for rapid control of specific responses, more precise input to the principal neurons is needed from other sources. The cortex is a major source of excitatory input but, as mentioned earlier, its effect may depend to a large extent on learning. Paths carrying innately rewarding stimuli reach the striatum via the hypothalamus and amygdala, probably synapsing mainly with the response-releasing direct path neurons.

Aversive stimuli are transmitted through similar routes, as well as via the *centre median* and parafascicular nuclei of the thalamus. Aversive afferents to the striatum are assumed to have innate connections to indirect-path (ENK) neurons, inhibiting centrally generated responses.

These inputs from the amygdala and diencephalon support the specific consummatory and escape responses to rewarding and punishing stimuli by enabling and disabling the release of responses in a more well-defined and precisely timed way than may be achieved by the dopamine input. In emergencies, reinforcers may determine responses through direct brainstem and spinal reflexes that completely bypass basal ganglia control.

CONDITIONED REINFORCEMENT

Stimuli can be divided roughly into three innately determined categories: consistently rewarding, consistently aversive, and the rest. As we have just seen, the rest are often initially aversive and then temporarily rewarding, but they lack the connections that prevent these qualities from disappearing with prolonged exposure. They may, however, acquire rewarding or aversive properties by association with activity evoked by stimuli that are consistently rewarding or aversive.

For example, after training during which rewards are accompanied by one sound, and lack of reward is accompanied by a different sound, monkeys can learn new visual discriminations rewarded or punished only by the sounds (Gaffan & Harrison, 1987), much as human beings can be rewarded and punished by words meaning "right" and "wrong."

In short, plans to make responses that evoke the sound associated with reward are released to the motor system, but plans to make responses that evoke the other sound are inhibited. The amygdala is involved in this association of sound with reinforcing effect. Acquisition of the association is impaired either by amygdalectomy or by severing the amygdala's connection with the auditory system.

The simplest explanation for this type of learning is that food-reward signals are relayed to the striatum by the amygdala, and it is in the amygdala that the association between reward and sound takes place. Thus, for a time, the sound has an effect on planned responses similar to that of food.

Alternatively, it is possible that association takes place in the striatum. If rewarding input from the amygdala releases response plans, it probably excites medium spiny neurons of the direct path. Any sensory input such as a sound that reaches the striatum from the cortex at the same time as a reward, would acquire connections to the activated release mechanism. The sensory input thereby acquires the power to release response plans and thus behave as a reward.

In a simpler demonstration revealing the role of the amygdala, McDonald and White (1993) showed that normal rats quickly acquire a preference for a place where they have found food, but amygdalectomized rats do not. Rats also acquire a preference for a place where they have experienced the effect of amphetamine. This preference is diminished by an injection of neuroleptic into the nucleus accumbens or a lesion of the lateral nucleus of the amygdala (Hiroi & White, 1991). This implies that input to the accumbens from the lateral nucleus of the amygdala is important for conditioned reward. When the rat is not in the place where it was rewarded, a plan to go there is associated with response disinhibition. Once the rat is there, a plan to leave receives no such assistance.

In a more recent experiment by Riedel, Harrington, Hall, and Macphail (1997), lesions of the nucleus accumbens greatly reduced the freezing behavior of rats in a chamber where they had experienced electric shocks. The lesions did not, however, reduce the freezing to a tone that was presented just before each shock. This suggests that the lesions eliminated input from the hippocampus to the striatum. The hippocampus is known to be important for spatial learning, and lesions there also impair place conditioning.

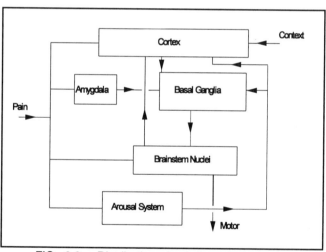

FIG. 9.2.   Distribution of pain input in the brain.

Input from the tone may enter the striatum via both the neocortex, and the amygdala.

Figure 9.2 is a diagram of how aversive connections might be organized according to the theory outlined earlier. Pain input, shown as having four branches, fires neurons that produce (a) arousal, (b) innate skeletal defensive responses, (c) innate limbic and striatal activity interpreted as emotional (e.g., anxiety, anger), and

(d) a neural representation of the pain stimulus in the cortex.

When all these activities are aroused, cortical representations of the pain and of contextual stimuli present at the same time, acquire strong connections with subcortical neurons involved in the accompanying emotional state. These include neurons responsible for fear responses such as fleeing or hiding that are expressed after the motor system ceases to be preempted by reflex responses such as vocalization and withdrawal that are elicited by the painful stimulus.

It is an oversimplification, but certainly plausible, to assume that fear and anxiety are accompanied by activity of striatal neurons of the indirect path, which inhibits responding, just as pleasure probably includes the firing of direct-path striatal neurons, which facilitates responding.

PASSIVE AVOIDANCE

According to the model under consideration, when an animal is hurt, input to the striatum from the thalamus and amygdala fires mainly enkephalin-containing neurons of the indirect path, setting them up to acquire an association with prevailing cortical input. Thus, the engrams of contextual stimuli present at about the time of the injury become associated with ongoing striatal activity via the cortico-striatal (including hippocampal-striatal) paths. Subsequently, if the animal finds itself in the same surroundings, the engrams representing the sensory input fire the indirect striatal path with which they have become associated, and locomotor responses are suppressed. Any plan to approach a place where pain has been experienced is thereby inhibited.

INSTRUMENTAL REWARD LEARNING

When a reward is presented, the theory suggests that the direct path striatal cells are fired, probably by input from the hypothalamus and amygdala, augmented by dopamine release. Therefore, it is with neurons of the direct path that the cortical representation of the reward and its contextual stimuli become associated. Release of excess dopamine in the striatum also may reinforce and accelerate the synaptic changes involved in establishing these associations (Beninger, 1983; White & Milner, 1992).

Obviously, when an experienced rat approaches and presses a lever to obtain water or brain stimulation, it is not the reward itself (which the rat has not yet perceived) that motivates the behavior. The lever might have been attractive the first few times it was encountered, because of its novelty, but it would not attract an experienced rat had it not been associated with a reward. Instrumental responses are released, and probably instigated, by environmental stimuli that have acquired connections with neurons in the striatum that initially were fired only by innately rewarding stimuli.

The Skinner box presents opportunities for adopting any number of response plans, each promising a different outcome. The expectancy model predicts that of the various plans, the one whose outcome has the strongest association with the concept of a reward (after any aversive associations have been subtracted) is the one most likely to be executed.

The neural activity that most consistently precedes the presentation of a reward is the one corresponding to the response plan that, in the context of the Skinner box, generates a successful response. Recording studies (Alexander & Crutcher, 1990b; Kimura, Rajkowski, & Evarts, 1984) indicate that when an animal prepares to make a response, neural activity increases throughout a loop that includes the frontal cortex, the basal ganglia, and the thalamus (black arrows in fig. 9.3).

When bar pressing is frequently rewarded, the component of the response planning activity in the frontal cortex acquires association with neurons of the lever

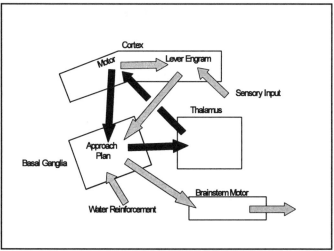

FIG. 9.3.   Intention loop linking cortex, basal ganglia, and thalamus during response planning.

engram. Thus, when the plan to press the lever is active, attention is directed to the lever. At the same time, the striatal component of the plan becomes associated with response-releasing neurons in the basal ganglia fired by the reward.

Subsequently, whenever internal osmoreceptors indicate the need for water, for example, activity is aroused in response-planning loops related to drinking. The cortical component of these activities then facilitates, via descending attention pathways, the engrams of stimuli related to drinking, including the lever of a Skinner box that can deliver water.

If any such object is present, its sensory input is intensified by the attentional facilitation, with the result that a stronger signal is delivered to the striatum. If there are several such objects, the one with the strongest association to a thirst-quenching response plan assumes control of the loop. In the present example, this object probably would be the Skinner-box lever, toward which the animal then advances.

Attentional facilitation of the lever engram is relayed back, as described in chapter 4, to earlier levels of the visual system, including the superior colliculus.

This further amplifies the visual input from the lever and ensures that the image of the lever is held in central vision. Intensified retinotopic activity containing information about the location of the lever is delivered to the motor cortex via the dorsal visual pathway. This supplies missing details required by the response plan, so that the lever, and not some other object, is approached and manipulated. Meanwhile, the stronger sensory input to the striatum increases the pre-response activity around the motor loop until its effect on the motor release pathway is sufficiently intense to allow the planned response to occur.

CONDITIONED BRAIN STIMULATION REWARD

Brain stimulation reward is a special case of motivation because, at the outset, there is no central activity that signals a need for it. Nevertheless, a naive rat with an electrode in its medial forebrain bundle vigorously presses a Skinner-box lever that delivers brain stimulation on first encountering it. The next day, however, the rat may take just as long to approach the lever as it did on the earlier occasion.

The first bar press is presumably accidental, perhaps an attempt to climb onto the lever. But the resulting burst of medial forebrain bundle stimulation produces an immediate lowering of the response threshold, so that the response is likely to be repeated. The excess dopamine that quickly builds up in the striatum prevents the response plan from habituating, or extinguishing, so responding continues at a high rate throughout the session.

The onset of the dopamine facilitation is rapid, but it disappears again after a few minutes when stimulation is discontinued. On the next day, the sight of the lever from a distance, and plans to approach and press it, are unlikely to be associated with the response-release mechanism strongly enough to give the approach response any significant advantage over other exploratory responses. Thus, despite the animal's apparent avidity after having received a burst of stimulation, it may take several brain-stimulation sessions over a period of days to produce the long-lasting synaptic changes needed to ensure that the animal goes promptly to the lever at the beginning of a new session and starts to press it.

THE NEURAL BASIS OF EXTINCTION

It is easy to think of simple ways in which rewards might encourage learning. Thorndike (1931), for example, thought that satisfaction was the cement that attached stimuli to responses, a function now more often attributed to dopamine. Cognitive psychologists assume that rewards establish expectations. Both of these processes may well be important (Milner, 1957; White & Milner, 1992). More severe theoretical difficulties arise when a reward fails to materialize, ungluing Thorndike's connections, and dashing expectations.

Introspection suggests that during extinction we do not forget that a response was at one time rewarded or punished, we remember that it no longer is. There is no reason to believe that monkeys and rats behave differently. Recently extinguished behavior usually re-appears spontaneously after an interval with no further trials. (The animal forgets, or ignores the less consolidated new learning.) Responding is restored very rapidly whenever reinforcement is reintroduced. After several cycles of extinction and reinforcement, the animal's response often extinguishes after one unreinforced trial and resumes after a single reinforcement. Reinforcement may contribute to the establishment of associations, but it is less important for maintaining them. Rather, its function appears to involve switching the dominant expectation, probably by a recency effect on relative synaptic strengths.

RECIPROCAL COUPLING OF REWARD AND PUNISHMENT

It is evident that failure to receive an expected reward is aversive (Tinkelpaugh, 1928), just as the opposite, failure to receive an expected punishment, is a cause for elation. This could be the result of reciprocal inhibitory connections between reward and punishing striatal pathways. If that is the case, as activity in one system collapses, a burst of activity would be released in the other (Grossberg & Levine, 1987).

In terms of the model under discussion, extinction does not destroy an association between a stimulus and the plan to perform an instrumental response, nor the association between the plan to produce a response and the response-release mechanism. Instead, extinction establishes an additional association between the response plan and the rebound response inhibition that occurs when the predicted reward is not received.

This new association of the response plan eventually becomes strong enough to overcome its original association with response release. However, new synaptic connections, always predominantly via soft synapses, decay more quickly than long-established connections. Therefore, after a period of disuse, the more recent association weakens and can no longer override the older one. The expectation of reward "spontaneously" reasserts itself but, of course, if there is still no reinforcement, the inhibitory association soon is refreshed. If reinforcement is reintroduced, however, the short-term increase in associative strength in the response-release circuit quickly restores normal responding.

Most rewarding stimuli activate the response release mechanism via subcortical pathways, but because the stimuli also establish neural representations in the cortex, an association soon develops between the representation and the response release mechanism. This association is temporarily strengthened each time the reward appears, even if it is presented outside the context of the learning situation. Thus, even a non-contingent reward can hasten the recovery of an extinguished response.

ACTIVE AVOIDANCE

Active avoidance has always presented difficulties for behavior theory, especially neural theories. If punishment has a generally inhibitory effect on intentional responses, how can a stimulus associated with punishment release an avoidance response? Reciprocal connections between the response release and inhibition paths in the striatum might be the answer. When an animal escapes from an aversive situation by the exercise of a withdrawal reflex, or an instinctive response organized at the brainstem level, the contextual stimuli after the escape become associated with the rebound activity of the response release path. Thus, although stimuli present during the punishment acquire an association with an aversive emotional state, stimuli present after a successful escape acquire rewarding associations and become attractive.

DISCRIMINATION

It is inevitable that some engrams of unreinforced stimuli should overlap the engram of a reinforced stimulus. When the overlap is large, the incorrect stimulus has an effect similar to the correct stimulus on the response-planning and response-releasing mechanisms, resulting in an error. For an animal to learn to discriminate between the reinforced and an overlapping unreinforced stimulus, the response to the incorrect stimulus must be extinguished without also extinguishing the response to the correct stimulus.

If a dog confuses its food dish with a slightly different dish that contains no food, each time it makes an error the neurons representing the empty dish (including those that also fire during presentation of the correct dish) acquire connections with the rebounding response inhibitory system, as described in earlier sections. As a result, the overlapping neurons, those fired by both correct and incorrect stimuli, are eventually connected to both response-releasing and response-inhibitory systems, reducing their reinforcing effectiveness.

Neurons fired only by the unreinforced stimulus have no response-release associations. They acquire connections only with the response inhibitory system. Therefore, if the overlap is not too great, these neurons soon overwhelm any residual release effect of the neurons fired by both stimuli, and the animal stops responding to the incorrect dish.

Neurons fired only by the correct stimulus, and not by the empty dish, acquire no connections to the inhibitory system. They continue to be connected only to the response-release mechanism. Whenever the correct dish is presented they release the response despite the reduced effectiveness of the neurons fired by both dishes. The animal thus responds only to the rewarded stimulus.

The greater the amount of overlap between the neurons fired by the rewarded and unrewarded stimuli, the fewer the neurons on which the correct response hinges, and the more likely the animal is to fail, or the longer it will take for the discrimination to be acquired.

Often the situation is more complicated than indicated in the preceding account, because of changes in attention. Our hypothetical dog usually appears to concentrate its attention on the dishes, ignoring the large number of stimuli in the room that have no close association with food. When the false dish is introduced, the dog attends to it as closely as if it were the food dish. However, as the elements it has in common with the food dish acquire associations that cancel their positive associations, these elements take on the characteristics of other neutral contextual stimuli such as the surrounding furniture. They lose their attention getting property. The dog's attention is now captured by the non-overlapping stimuli, those that signify food or no food.

As proposed in chapter 1, sensory neurons receive attentional facilitation from their association with motivational activity. Many of the sensory neurons fired by the false dish have their association with food canceled, and thus no longer receive attentional facilitation. Those fired only by false-dish stimuli acquire attentional connections with punishment and avoidance responses. When the dog is planning to approach food, attentional facilitation is directed only to the non-overlapping characteristics that distinguish the correct and incorrect dishes.

The engram of a stimulus becomes more refined as the stimulus is experienced in different response contexts. Initially, the concept of "square" may include any four-sided figure, but eventually neurons fired by parallelograms, rectangles, trapeziums, and other quadrilateral figures are eliminated from the concept.

SUMMARY

Among the many functions of the basal ganglia, modulation of the motor threshold is one of the more conspicuous. This function plays an essential part in an expectancy theory of learning, releasing or inhibiting planned responses according to their predicted outcomes. Responses whose outcomes cannot be predicted usually escape inhibition, probably because their planning does not produce an increase of cortical input to the striatum. Thus, novelty has an effect similar to that of reward, enabling animals to explore and add to their stock of cognitive relationships.

Responses that usually lead to rewards continue to be released even though their outcome is predictable. It is postulated that rewarding stimuli have innate (mostly subcortical) connections to striatal mechanisms for response release. Cortical input to the striatum during reward acquires associations with the response- releasing mechanism, thereby acquiring motivational properties. Increased dopaminergic activity is one of the mechanisms supporting response release. It also may promote the formation of direct associations between cortical input to the striatum and the response-releasing circuit.

Punishing stimuli have innate connections to mechanisms in the striatum for inhibiting voluntary responses. (Responses to severe punishment are usually reflexive or instinctive, and are mostly organized at a spinal or brainstem level below that of the basal ganglia.) Cortical input to the striatum is associated with the response inhibition that accompanies punishment, resulting in conditioned avoidance.

Self-stimulation of the brain that releases dopamine in the striatum appears to be highly rewarding because it is acquired very quickly. This may be a false impression resulting from a lowering of the response threshold by dopamine. After a pause of a few minutes to allow the dopamine level to return to normal, the animal's interest in the situation is much reduced. Only after a number of sessions does the sight of the manipulandum immediately attract the animal.

It is easy to demonstrate a reciprocal relationship between reward and punishment. A disappointed reward expectancy is punishing, and vice versa. This suggests that the response-releasing and response-inhibitory systems inhibit each other, with rebound hyperactivity of either system occurring whenever there is a rapid decline of inhibition from the other. This would explain why animals cease to make responses that are no longer rewarded, and learn to make responses that remove them from a punishing or frightening situation.

This reciprocal inhibition of antagonist motivation systems also can explain how animals learn to discriminate between reinforced and unreinforced stimuli with similar characteristics. Any neuron fired by a reinforced stimulus may acquire an association with a response-releasing or response-inhibitory mechanism, but in the case of neurons that are fired also by unreinforced stimuli, this association is eventually annulled by an association with the opposing system. Discrimination also involves changes in the way attention influences neural representations of objects.

10 Envoi

Probably the most unfortunate effect on psychology of the behaviorist revolution was its suppression of mental concepts such as ideas and images. In 1890 William James could give the title *The Stream of Thought* to a chapter of his influential textbook, *The Principles of Psychology*. In it he wrote: "The first fact for us, as psychologists, is that thinking of some sort goes on" (p. 224). A few years later, no theoretical psychologist who valued his or her reputation would have dared to mention such topics. For the next 30 or 40 years only stimuli were allowed to influence behavior (Watson, 1919). In 1949, Hebb earned a place in the Psychological Hall of Fame by providing a neural basis for the idea, thereby giving it a new lease on life.

The cell assembly was such a good idea that it was embraced with enthusiasm despite its somewhat shaky neurological foundations; it signaled a great advance in behavior theory. The neural mechanism of the cell assembly is of secondary importance to psychologists, which is probably why the model has not been more seriously challenged, but the neurology is important if a true bridge between behavior and the nervous system is to be established.

Hebb himself recognized that the process of acquiring cell assemblies would have to be lengthy, and found a couple of observations that appeared to be in agreement with this prediction. Chimpanzees and human infants raised without vision never acquire normal vision if sight is restored later (Riesen, 1947; von Senden, 1932). Recent studies indicate, however, that under normal conditions the vision of human infants is surprisingly good within hours of birth (Kaye & Bower, 1994; Meltzoff & Moore, 1989; Walton & Bower, 1993).

BRITISH EMPIRICISM: AMERICAN OVERENTHUSIASM

Traditionally, American psychologists have been more sympathetic to empiricism than have other life scientists. Opposition to any suggestion of inborn ability reached a ridiculous level during the 1920s and 1930s during Hebb's student years. Lashley's (1938, 1947) generally nativist viewpoint had little effect on Hebb's empiricist bias despite the many years they spent working together. Ironically, Lashley's (1929) belief in the equipotentiality of the cortex may have had the opposite effect, contributing to the major role Hebb assigned to learning in the formation of cell assemblies.

The success of the cell assembly undoubtedly helped to solidify the widely held view that sensory input molds concepts from a formless brain matrix. Hebb did not hesitate to postulate a visual cortex with initially random connections, an assumption no present-day behavioral neuroscientist would be likely to make. The alternative view advanced in this monograph is that concepts are learned when activity of a highly organized inborn response system coincides with activity in the sensory systems.

It is further proposed that the main ascending sensory pathways are just that; pathways that with normal nourishment and stimulation provide connections between receptors and innately determined patterns of cortical neurons. Equally important is a collection of descending pathways that adjust the sensitivity of the ascending paths in accordance with intentions established by motivational and response planning systems.

Newborn infants of many species, including our own, can direct attention to specific stimuli, a process that requires the ascending and descending sensory systems to work together in a coordinated way. It is inconceivable that the required coordination could be established overnight, starting from a system completely lacking in organization.

Neural concepts can be active in the absence of the stimuli they represent. Cell assemblies are postulated to achieve this property by reverberating, a difficult process to control, and one that has resisted all efforts at computer simulation in any functional form. Damage to activating pathways in the brainstem results in unconsciousness and the cessation or significant reduction of cortical activity. In other words, concepts cannot maintain themselves in isolated cortex as might be expected of Hebb's reverberating loops.

The alternative proposed here has no intrinsic mechanism for producing or maintaining activity. Sensory input is stored briefly by chemical processes at synapses that link the trace to an external source of drive activity, probably derived from the response planning mechanism. This hypothesis is easier to investigate and is supported by recent neuroanatomical mapping and microelectrode recording.

The group of neurons representing a concept may thus be activated either by innate connections from sensory input or by mostly learned links with a complicated activation mechanism that includes motivation, response planning, and possibly brainstem arousal activity. The durations of the links formed between concept neurons and these sources of activation range from a few seconds to many years depending on the synapses involved and on the number of times the concepts are invoked.

In the absence of sensory input the neurons fire when they are stimulated by an intention, not when they feel like reverberating. They have a specific function which is to allow the motor system to recruit, via attention, stimulation that has proved valuable during previous attempts to carry out an intention.

SENSORY PATHWAYS

In olfaction, a primitive sense, there are several hundred different types of receptor, most of them sensitive to a range of chemical stimuli. From the anatomy of the system it seems likely that many different combinations of their outputs converge on neurons in various subcortical nuclei and in the olfactory cortex. The theoretical number of possible combinations is truly astronomical, of the order of 10^{100}, but obviously the number in actual use is limited by the number of neurons in the receiving areas. Animals presumably are biased to inherit connections activated by odors of special significance to them.

In the visual system, the same sort of convergences take place. Axon terminals carrying information from a group of receptors, typically occupying a narrow strip, converge on a single cortical neuron, which therefore responds most strongly to a line of light that falls on most of the receptors in the group. The neuron also fires, though less strongly, if the line is at an angle to the optimum orientation. This makes it impossible to tell, by looking at the output of a single cortical neuron, exactly where the stimulating line is, or even if it is a line. Precise perception depends on being able to compare the activities of many neurons, to determine which are being fired most strongly.

After several more layers of convergence, neurons that respond to complex shapes are to be found in the inferotemporal visual cortex. As at the earlier levels of the visual cortex, the information provided by the firing of a single neuron is ambiguous. To determine what shape is present, all the neurons being fired must be taken into account. It is likely that if a collection of cortical neurons has acquired a meaning (i.e., has become associated with a particular emotion or motivation, for example), other patterns that include a majority of the same neurons will initially have a similar meaning.

If for some reason that meaning is incorrect (it may be a skunk, not a squirrel), differences between the two patterns of cortical neurons become important. Neurons fired by skunks acquire one set of motivational and emotional associations, neurons fired by squirrels acquire different associations. Thus neurons fired by both animals acquire both sets of associations. To the extent that they are incompatible these associations contribute little to ensuing responses.

BEHAVIOR

The response mechanism, which involves motivational, emotional and motor activity, comprises a group of mutually inhibitory divisions. One is either afraid or secure, happy or sad; one approaches or retreats. If several incompatible responses or emotions are being aroused simultaneously, the one receiving most excitation will become active and suppress the rest. The non-overlapping parts of the skunk and squirrel engrams thus have the deciding vote on what response should be made. Human beings, of course, have names for most objects they encounter. As a result, even if the emotions and motivations aroused by two objects are similar, the engrams of the objects may still become associated with entirely different verbal responses.

Frequently, patterns of neural activity are associated with both a specific and a more general name. For example, dogs are also animals. Presumably, more of the neurons activated by dogs are associated with the name "animal" than with the name "dog". The group would include neurons also fired by cats, horses, iguanas, cod and dinosaurs.

A patient undergoing brain surgery became aphasic when his left temporal cortex was being electrically stimulated and was unable to name the picture of a butterfly. When the stimulation was removed, he remarked that he had not been able to think of "butterfly" and had tried, unsuccessfully, to remember "moth" instead (Penfield & Roberts, 1959). Clearly a concept of lepidoptera was active in his brain, but it had no access to any of the verbal responses normally associated with it.

SELECTIVE ATTENTION AND THE ENGRAM

Chapter 3 introduced the idea that neurons fired by a stimulus do not constitute an engram of that stimulus unless they have acquired connections from an affective state or a response plan of some kind. A motivational state usually has innate connections to neurons fired by stimuli that can satisfy the need. A thirsty animal needs water, for example, and at least one path sensitive to stimuli from water is innately facilitated by the motivation. If water is present, the activity in the path is intensified and selected to guide the behavior required to approach the water and drink.

This innate mechanism may be subcortical, but whenever it is activated, it gives rise to associations between the active motivational and motor mechanisms and some of the cortical neurons fired by water stimuli. These neurons constitute an engram for water. An engram is thus a collection of sensory neurons that can be facilitated by an intention or a motivation. Not all the neurons fired by a stimulus are incorporated into its engram, only those that acquire an association with the intention mechanism. Engram neurons, once established, are normally facilitated by the plan to make a response.

It has been clear for some time that the behavioral bottleneck is narrowest at the level of responding. There is nothing to prevent many different sensory inputs from being processed at the same time, but responses usually must compete with each other for the use of the musculature. R. Miller and Wickens (1991) must have had the same idea when they suggested that cell assemblies extend into the basal ganglia, where the competition between them occurs. In fact, apart from its retention of the reverberatory cell assembly, their model is quite similar to that described here.

The proposed model requires response plans to have learning synapses on all engram neurons. People have an extensive repertoire of gestures and vocalizations, far more than other animals. An impossibly large number of learning synapses per neuron would be required to allow instant associations to be established directly between any pair of them.

A possible solution to the problem (Chapter 3) might be for a number of sensory cortex neurons to be connected in parallel to form a "super neuron" with the required very large input capacity. The neurons that make up super neurons are not interconnected to form loops, as are the neurons in cell assemblies. They do not fire each other, but their outputs converge onto one or a few output neurons. In sensory cortex, neurons are arranged in columns, within which most of the neurons respond to similar stimuli (Tanaka, 1992). One function of these columns may be to increase the potential input capacity of neurons that represent a particular stimulus.

Once associations have been established between a response plan and some of the cortical neurons fired by stimuli present at about the time the response is made, these neurons (engram neurons) are excited by any subsequent intention to perform the response. Feedback of this induced engram activity to more peripheral levels of the sensory paths constitutes attention. The feedback facilitates neurons of the path, sensitizing them to the required stimuli. The sensory signals selected by the facilitation are delivered to the motor system, where they release and guide the planned response.

The attentional feedback from the active engram to more peripheral parts of the sensory paths facilitates, but normally does not fire the neurons there. It merely intensifies any activity already taking place. In this, it differs from the feedback assumed to be responsible for reverberating cell assemblies. The cell assemblies were thus postulated to become spontaneously active and produce effects similar to the stimuli they represent.

A long-standing puzzle is that a stimulus may acquire hundreds of different associations over the years, yet always seems to activate only the association most appropriate to the situation. This mystery is a consequence of the prevailing stimulus driven psychological theory. If we recognize that associations between concepts depend on the central executive system of the brain, not the sensory input, the mystery evaporates.

Two alternative mechanisms have been proposed to explain the transmission of attentional information from engrams to the peripheral sensory apparatus and the sensory-motor guidance paths. One suggestion (Milner, 1974) was that the information passed via recurrent paths, guided by the sensory impulses ascending along parallel paths in the opposite direction. Alternatively it has been suggested that all the neurons fired by a stimulus, including those of its engram, discharge synchronously (Singer & Gray, 1995). Thus, if the engram activity were to be fed back to coincidence detectors for comparison with sensory input, only those sensory impulses related to the engram would be selected. These impulses could then be forwarded to the motor system. Although this may appear to be a relatively precarious mechanism, requiring an improbable degree of temporal precision in all sensory pathways, it has some support from neurophysiological experiments (Roelfsema et al., 1997).

RECOGNITION

Many stimuli are not associated in any way with a reinforcer and therefore do not acquire connections with innately induced responses. Almost every stimulus is, however, innately reinforcing when it is first presented. As suggested in chapter 9, the first few times that neurons in the sensory cortices fire they activate an alerting mechanism, but instead of this connection being strengthened by use, the opposite occurs. This effect may be the result of learned inhibitory feedback that eventually disables the path to the alerting mechanism.

Many different combinations of sensory afferents, some of them infrequently or never used, converge on cortical neurons. Thus, a novel combination of sensory elements (even if the elements themselves are familiar) fires neurons that have never before fired, and whose path to the alerting system has not yet acquired effective inhibitory connections. Because of the arousal produced by novel stimuli, the cortical firing they evoke is intensified, producing an attention-like effect. Sensory input from the novel stimulus is enhanced by the facilitation, and the alarm path may incorporate a mechanism for fear expression. If, however, numerous familiar stimuli also are present, they could raise the threshold of the alerting system. At a lower level of arousal fear is attenuated allowing expression of investigatory behavior, another innate effect of arousal shown by many animals in novel situations.

The arousal produced by a novel object has a widespread effect on the nervous system. People learn to interpret this internal state as indicating the presence of something unfamiliar. Suppression of the arousal when habituation to a stimulus has occurred gives rise to cortical activity that identifies the stimulus as familiar. Thus, when a cortical representation of novelty or of familiarity is active at the same time as the engram of an object, the corresponding property is attributed to the object.

A pattern of sensory neurons that has been active sufficiently often to have acquired inhibitory connections to the alerting system may be recognized as familiar even though, when it is not present, it cannot be recalled. To be recalled it must have acquired associations from intentional, emotional or some other central activity. Until a pattern is associated with an internal state it cannot be regarded as a complete engram.

TIME AND THE ENGRAM

Percepts are rarely static. Although Hebb (1949) assigned dynamic characteristics to his cell assemblies, it is difficult to imagine how the intrinsic dynamics attributed to cell assemblies would keep in step with the arbitrary dynamics exhibited by most external stimuli.

The dynamic percepts chosen for discussion in chapter 5 were words. A polysyllabic word consists of several sounds delivered in a particular order over a short period. It is clear that to be interpreted as a unitary stimulus, the effects of all the sounds must merge. The trace of the first sound must continue to have an influence at least until the rest of the sounds have been heard.

There is no shortage of possible neural processes by which the effect of a stimulus may be preserved for a short time. Ion channels of the stimulated neuron may remain open for some time after the end of the stimulus, or the neuron may acquire a temporary association with a "clock" input that continues to fire it.. It may deliver signals (excitatory and inhibitory) that have persistent effects on the activity or sensitivity of other neurons. It is probable that a number of short-term synaptic processes contribute to the temporal integration of stimuli.

The order of the elements must be taken into account in an engram of a sequence of stimuli. The most obvious way in which this may be achieved is for the earlier elements to influence the way the later elements are processed. Thus, *b* at the beginning of a sequence modifies different synapses from those modified when the *b* follows an *a*, for example. The final pattern of synaptic changes depends on the elements, and on their sequential order. Once assembled, the pattern itself is static. It would not be easy to determine the original sequence from it. Nevertheless, it represents the dynamic stimulus just as other engrams may be static representations of complex spatial patterns.

A more interesting and difficult question is how sequential motor patterns are stored, specifically, how we learn to pronounce a word we hear. The problem is that a modest number of phonemes can be arranged to produce a mathematically limitless number of different sequences. If pronunciation of the word "apple" were to involve the association of "a" with "p" and "p" with "l," and so on, then how could the word "appear" be learned without destroying the word "apple"? Clearly, the engram of the word must exert some influence over the associations throughout the pronunciation.

The problems get worse. People can repeat a sequence of sounds they have heard only once. As the sounds were occurring, no engram could have existed because it requires all the elements for its formation. One way out of this dilemma is to store the sequence on a re-usable timebase until it can be stored more permanently by elements reserved by the engram for that particular word or sequence. The temporary timebase storage is what we know as rehearsal.

The timebase envisaged is really a virtual timebase consisting of decaying traces of the individual elements. The first sound facilitates the response plan capable of producing a similar sound and then immediately inhibits it. It is the fading of the inhibitory trace that determines when it will reappear. The second sound is treated similarly, therefore its trace takes the same length of time to recover from inhibition, emerging just after the first sound has done so. Subsequent elements also remain blanked out for a short period and recover in the order in which they were stored (though it is not unheard of for the phonemes of a strange word to be repeated in the wrong order at the first attempt.)

In this type of sequential storage, the elements are not associated with each other. They are plunged independently into silence as they occur, resurfacing after a fixed delay. This is a short-term solution to the problem of storing sequences. The elements can be repeatedly refreshed and re-inhibited, as during rehearsal, but once another stimulus diverts attention the elements return to baseline and may be recruited by some other sound sequence. If the original sequence has not been transferred in the meantime to a more permanent system, it is lost. As pointed out in Chapter 5, such a system must depend on the formation of an engram for the sequence during rehearsal. Once the engram has been acquired, it can isolate small samples of the neurons that represent the elemental sounds of the sequence, so that they can be associated with each other without interference from other sequences that contain similar elements.

MEMORY

So far in this chapter, we have discussed mostly utilitarian synaptic modifications. These changes allow more effective attainment of goals. When or how they were produced is of little relevance to their purpose. The resulting behavior often is referred to as a habit, though it should be obvious that few, if any, habits can be explained by the simple association of stimulus with response, as some psychologists still apparently believe.

The term "memory" is most often applied to specific events that have been stored and recalled. In animals with effective social communication, such as ants, bees, and human beings, this type of memory also can be utilitarian. Information gathered at a remote time and place can be made available to other members of the community.

The usual method of testing memory in humans is to present new information and measure its recall at various intervals later. However, even with no incentive to remember, the average person automatically retains an enormous amount of information during the course of a day. Depending largely on the intensity of emotion aroused by an event it may be forgotten within minutes or remembered for life.

The same is true of animals. According to myth, elephants never forget being harshly treated, and it is always good insurance to take thorns out of a lion's paw when the opportunity arises, in case, like Androcles, you meet the animal again in an arena. Better authenticated observations reveal that rats persistently avoid places where they have received a strong electric shock, though it is not known whether they lie awake thinking about the frightening experience when they are away from the scene. In other words, can they remember the event, or has it just produced a change in their response to a context or other stimulus? Is it episodic memory or one-trial learning?

Examples of long-term memory in animals tend to be highly specific. At spawning time, salmon return to the stream they left years before, guided by an imprinted memory of its odor. Some migrating birds return to their nesting sites after wintering thousands of miles away. Other species hide food and find it again months later. It is doubtful, however, whether these performances reflect a process comparable to human episodic memory, which is not at all specific, nor necessarily so beneficial.

A striking feature of episodic memory is that the same object often features in many different memories. If you own a car you probably see it almost every day in a number of different places. Your memory of where it is parked today is quite separate from your memory of it yesterday, though both presumably involve activating the engram of the car. Later these memories are remembered as memories, not as experiences of the actual car. Hence, when an engram is fired by sensory input, neurons must be fired that do not fire when the engram is fired by association with some central activity such as a response plan. Even so, it is not likely that neurons in the peripheral part of the sensory path enter importantly into episodic memory associations. If they did, hallucinations might be expected to accompany the memory.

The fact that we can usually remember where an object was when last seen may be explained by the prevalence of "place" neurons in the hippocampus (O'Keefe & Dostrovsky, 1971; O'Keefe & Nadel, 1978; Wilson & McNaughton, 1993), and probably in neocortical areas also. These neurons continuously provide information about the location of surrounding objects in relation to the body, and are available at all times to form associations with the neurons of active engrams.

The mechanism for recording when you last saw the object is even more speculative. In fact, there must be several mechanisms, depending on how long ago it was. For short intervals, an estimate relative to the present is probably the most useful. Such an estimate could be derived from the strength of the associations at the time the memory is recovered. The longer the interval, the fewer will be the number of synaptic changes that remain effective. This mechanism might be useful for periods of up to a few hours.

For longer periods, named indicators of the time, such as "mid-morning," or "about ten o'clock," might be more appropriate than an estimate relative to the present. In the absence of external cues, neurons driven by the circadian clock could provide time relative to the day - night cycle. Seasonal changes or calendar dates provide associations for even longer intervals. Every event that is noticed and remembered must produce a trace whose associations not only identify the participating objects, but also the surroundings and the time it occurred relative to a variety of markers. The engram may not be as complicated as Hebb (1949) imagined, but it is far from simple.

The engram properties that have been discussed in the chapters of this book do not entirely rule out the possibility that engrams are arbitrary assemblies of neurons that chance experiences have brought together to form reverberating loops, but in my view they come close to doing so.

Bibliography

Adams, R. D., Collins, G. H., & Victor, M. (1962). Troubles de la mémoire et de l'apprentissage chez l'homme; leurs relations avec des lésions des lobes temporaux et du diencéphale. In P. Passouant. (Ed.), *Physiologie de l'hippocampe*. (pp. 273-291). Paris: Centre Nationale de Recherche Scientifique.

Alexander, G. E., & Crutcher, M. D. (1990a). Functional architecture of basal ganglia circuits: neural substrates of parallel processing. *Trends in Neurosciences, 13*, 266-271.

Alexander, G. E., & Crutcher, M. D. (1990b). Preparation for movement: Neural representations of intended direction in three motor areas of the monkey. *Journal of Neurophysiology, 64*, 133-150.

Alexander, G. E., DeLong, M. R., & Strick, P. L. (1986). Parallel organization of functionally segregated circuits linking basal ganglia and cortex. *Annual Review of Neuroscience, 9*, 357-381.

Alvarez, P., & Squire, L. R. (1994). Memory consolidation and the medial temporal lobe: A simple network model. *Proceedings of the National Academy of Sciences U.S.A., 91*, 7041-7045.

Amit, D. J. (1995). The Hebbian paradigm reintegrated: Local reverberations as internal representations. *Behavioral and Brain Sciences, 18*, 617-657.

Baddeley, A. (1992). Working memory. *Science, 255*, 556-559.

Barlow, H. B. (1972). Single units and sensation: A neuron doctrine for perceptual psychology? *Perception, 1*, 371-394.

Bear, M. F. (1997). How do memories leave their mark? *Nature, 385*, 481-482.

Bekhterev, V. M. (1900). Demonstration eines Gehirns mit Zerstörung der vorderen und inneren Theile der Hirnrinde beider Schläfenlappen. *Neurologische Zeitenblatte, 19*, 990-991.

Beninger, R. J. (1983). The role of dopamine in locomotor activity and learning. *Brain Research Reviews, 6*, 173-196.

Beninger, R. J., Cheng, M., Hahn, B. L., Hoffman, D. C., Mazurski, E. J., Morency, M. A., Ramm, P., & Stewart, R. J. (1987). Effects of extinction, pimozide, SCH 23390, and metoclopramide on food-rewarded operant responding of rats. *Psychopharmacology, 92*, 343-349.

Bianchi, L. (1895). The functions of the frontal lobes. *Brain, 18*, 497-522.

Bickford, R. G., Mulder, D. W., Dodge, H. W., Svien, H. J., & Rome, H. P. (1958). Changes in memory function produced by electrical stimulation of the temporal lobe in man. *Research Publications of the Association for Research in Nervous and Mental Disease, 36*, 227-243.

Biederman, I. (1987). Recognition by components: A theory of human image understanding. *Psychological Review, 94*, 115-147.

Bielajew, C., & Shizgal, P. (1986). Evidence implicating descending fibers in self-stimulation of the medial forebrain bundle. *Journal of Neuroscience, 6* (4), 919-929.

Blackburn, J. R., Phillips, A. G., Jakubovic, A., & Fibiger, H. C. (1986). Increased dopamine metabolism in the nucleus accumbens and striatum following consumption of a nutritive meal but not a palatable non-nutritive saccharin solution. *Pharmacology Biochemistry and Behavior, 25,* 1095-1100.

Blackburn, J. R., Phillips, A. G., Jakubovic, A., & Fibiger, H. C. (1989). Dopamine and preparatory behavior: II. A neurochemical analysis. *Behavioral Neuroscience, 103,* 15-23.

Bliss, T. V. P., & Lømo, T. (1970). Plasticity in a monosynaptic cortical pathway. *Journal of Physiology, 207,* 61P.

Block, N. (1996). How can we find the neural correlate of consciousness? *Trends in Neurosciences, 11,* 456-459.

Bolles, R. C. (1972). Reinforcement, expectancy and learning. *Psychological Review, 79,* 394-409.

Bozarth, M. A. (1987). Ventral tegmental reward system. In J. Engel & L. Oreland. (Eds.), *Brain reward systems and abuse.* (pp. 1-17). New York: Raven Press.

Brady, J. V., & Nauta, W. J. H. (1953). Subcortical mechanisms in emotional behavior: Affective changes following septal forebrain lesions in the albino rat. *Journal of Comparative and Physiological Psychology, 46,* 339-346.

Braitenberg, V. (1984). *Vehicles: Experiments in synthetic psychology.* Cambridge, MA: MIT Press.

Braitenberg, V. (1989). Some arguments for a theory of cell assemblies in the cerebral cortex. In L. Nadel, L. A. Cooper, P. Culicover, & R. M. Harnish. (Eds.), *Neural connections, mental computation.* (pp. 137-145). Cambridge, MA: MIT Press.

Breland, K., & Breland, M. (1961). The misbehavior of organisms. *American Psychologist, 16,* 681-684.

Broadbent, D. E. (1956). Successive responses to simultaneous stimuli. *Quarterly Journal of Experimental Psychology, 8,* 145-162.

Broekkamp, C. L. E. (1976). *The modulation of rewarding systems in the animal brain by amphetamine, morphine and apomorphine.* Nijmegen, Holland: Stichting Studentenpers.

Brown, S., & Schäfer, E. A. (1888). An investigation into the functions of the occipital and temporal lobes of the monkey's brain. *Philosophical Transactions of the Royal Society of London. Series B., 179,* 303-327.

Buck, L. B. (1996). Information coding in the vertebrate olfactory system. *Annual Review of Neuroscience, 19,* 517-544.

Butler, R. A. (1953). Discrimination learning by rhesus monkeys to visual-exploration motivation. *Journal of Comparative and Physiological Psychology, 46,* 95-98.

Castellucci, V. F., & Kandel, E. R. (1974). A quantal analysis of the synaptic depression underlying habituation of the gill-withdrawal reflex in *Aplysia. Proceedings of the National Academy of Sciences U.S.A., 71,* 5004-5008.

Chapman, L. F., Walter, R. D., Markham, C. H., Rand, R. W., & Crandall, P. H. (1967). Memory changes induced by stimulation of hippocampus or amygdala in epilepsy patients with implanted electrodes. *Transactions of the American Neurological Association, 92,* 50-56.

Chelazzi, L., Miller, E. K., Duncan, J., & Desimone, R. (1993). A neural basis for visual search in inferior temporal cortex. *Nature, 363,* 345-347.

Christopher, M. Sister, & Butter, C. M. (1968). Consummatory behaviors and locomotor exploration evoked from self-stimulation sites in rats. *Journal of Comparative and Physiological Psychology, 66,* 335-339.

Cohen, N. J., & Eichenbaum, H. (1993). *Memory, amnesia and the hippocampal system.* Cambridge, MA: MIT Press.

Cohen, N. J., & Squire, L. R. (1980). Preserved learning and retention of pattern-analysing skill in amnesia: Dissociation of knowing how and knowing that. *Science, 210,* 207-210.

Cools, A. R., & van Rossum, J. M. (1980). Multiple receptors for brain dopamine in behavior regulation: Concept of dopamine-E and dopamine-I receptors. *Life Sciences, 27,* 1237-1253.

Corkin, S. (1984). Lasting consequences of bilateral medial temporal lobectomy: Clinical course and experimental findings. *Seminars in Neurology, 4,* 249-259.

Corkin, S., Amaral, D. G., González, R. G., Johnson, K. A., & Hyman, B. T. (1997). H.M.'s medial temporal lobe lesion: Findings from magnetic resonance imaging. *Journal of Neuroscience*, *17*, 3964-3979.

Crick, F., & Koch, C. (1990). Towards a neurobiological theory of consciousness. *Seminars in the Neurosciences*, *2*, 263-275.

Dahlström, A., & Fuxe, K. (1964). Evidence for the existence of monoamine-containing neurons in the central nervous system. I. Demonstration of monoamine in the cell bodies of brain stem neurons. *Acta Physiologica Scandinavica*, *62*, Suppl. 232, 1-55.

Damsma, G., Pfaus, J. G., Wenkstern, D., Phillips, A. G., & Fibiger, H. C. (1992). Sexual behavior increases dopamine transmission in the nucleus accumbens and striatum of male rats: Comparison with novelty and locomotion. *Behavioral Neuroscience*, *106*, 181-191.

DeLong, M. R., Crutcher, M. D., & Georgopoulos, A. P. (1985). Primate globus pallidus and subthalamic nucleus: Functional organization. *Journal of Neurophysiology*, *53*, 530-543.

Descartes, R. (1955). *Les passions de l'âme*. Paris: J.Vrin.

Desimone, R., Albright, T. D., Gross, C. G., & Bruce, C. (1984). Stimulus-selective properties of inferior temporal neurons in the macaque. *Journal of Neuroscience*, *4*, 2051-2062.

Desimone, R., & Duncan, J. (1995). Neural mechanisms of selective visual attention. *Annual Review of Neuroscience*, *18*, 193-222.

DeYoe, E. A., & Van Essen, D. C. (1988). Concurrent processing streams in monkey visual cortex. *Trends in Neurosciences*, *11*, 219-226.

Dickinson, A., & Balleine, B. (1993). Actions and responses: The dual psychology of behavior. In N. Eilan, R. A. McCarthy, & M. W. Brewer. (Eds.), *Spatial representation: Problems in philosophy and psychology*. (pp. 277-293). Oxford: Blackwell.

Doty, R. W., & Bosma, J. F. (1956). An electromyographic analysis of reflex deglutition. *Journal of Neurophysiology*, *19*, 44-60.

Driesch, H. (1908). *Science and philosophy of the organism*. London: A.&C. Black.

Duncan, C. P. (1949). The retroactive effect of electroshock on learning. *Journal of Comparative and Physiological Psychology*, *42*, 32-44.

Dusoir, H., Kapur, N., Byrnes, D. P., McKinstry, S., & Hoare, R. D. (1990). The role of diencephalic pathology in human memory disorder. Evidence from a penetrating paranasal brain injury. *Brain*, *113*, 1695-1706.

Ebbinghaus, H. (1885). *Über das Gedächtnis*. Leipzig: Duncker & Humblot.

Eccles, J. C. (1953). *The neurophysiological basis of mind*. Oxford: Clarendon Press.

Eichenbaum, H., Otto, T., & Cohen, N. J. (1994). Two functional components of the hippocampal memory system. *Behavioral and Brain Sciences*, *17*, 449-518.

Elman, J. L. (1990). Finding structure in time. *Cognitive Science*, *14*, 179-211.

Engel, A. K., Roelfsema, P. R., Fries, P., Brecht, M., & Singer, W. (1997). Role of the temporal domain for response selection and perceptual binding. *Cerebral Cortex*, *7*, 571-582.

Ettenberg, A. (1989). Dopamine, neuroleptics and reinforced behavior. *Neuroscience and Biobehavioral Review*, *13*, 105-111.

Ettenberg, A., & Camp, C. H. (1986a). Haloperidol induces a partial reinforcement extinction effect in rats: Implications for a dopamine involvement in food reward. *Pharmacology Biochemistry and Behavior*, *25*, 813-821.

Ettenberg, A., & Camp, C. H. (1986b). A partial reinforcement extinction effect in water-reinforced rats intermittently treated with haloperidol. *Pharmacology Biochemistry and Behavior*, *25*, 1231-1235.

Ettenberg, A., & Duvauchelle, C. L. (1988). Haloperidol blocks the conditioned place preferences induced by rewarding brain stimulation. *Behavioral Neuroscience*, *102*, 687-691.

Ettenberg, A., & Milner, P. M. (1977). Effects of dopamine supersensitivity on lateral hypothalamic self-stimulation in rats. *Pharmacology Biochemistry and Behavior*, *7*, 507-514.

Everitt, B. J., Morris, K. A., O'Brien, A., & Robbins, T. W. (1991). The basolateral amygdala-ventral striatal system and conditioned place preference: Further evidence of limbic-striatal interactions underlying reward-related processes. *Neuroscience, 42*, 1-18.

Fallon, J. H., & Loughlin, S. E. (1985). Substantia nigra. In G. Paxinos. (Ed.), *The rat nervous system Vol 1.* (pp. 353-374). Sydney: Academic Press.

Feindel, W. (1961). Response patterns elicited from the amygdala and deep temperoinsular cortex. In D. E. Sheer. (Ed.), *Electrical stimulation of the brain.* (pp. 519-532). Austin: University of Texas Press.

Ford, L. M., Norman, A. B., & Sanberg, P. R. (1989). The topography of MK-801-induced locomotor patterns in rats. *Physiology and Behavior, 46*, 755-758.

Fouriezos, G., Hansson, P., & Wise, R. A. (1978). Neuroleptic-induced attenuation of brain stimulation reward in rats. *Journal of Comparative and Physiological Psychology, 92*, 661-671.

Fouriezos, G., & Wise, R. A. (1976). Pimozide-induced extinction of intracranial self-stimulation: Response patterns rule out motor or performance deficits. *Brain Research, 103*, 377-380.

French, G. M. (1959). Locomotor effects of regional ablations of frontal cortex in rhesus monkeys. *Journal of Comparative and Physiological Psychology, 52*, 18-24.

French, G. M., & Harlow, H. F. (1955). Locomotor reaction decrement in normal and brain-damaged monkeys. *Journal of Comparative and Physiological Psychology, 48*, 496-501.

Frey, U., & Morris, R. G. M. (1997). Synaptic tagging and long-term potentiation. *Nature, 385*, 533-536.

Frey, U., & Morris, R. G. M. (1998). Synaptic tagging: Implications for late maintenance of hippocampal long-term potentiation. *Trends in Neurosciences, 21*, 181-188.

Fuster, J. M. (1997). Network memory. *Trends in Neurosciences, 20*, 451-459.

Fuster, J. M., Bauer, R. H., & Jervey, J. P. (1985). Functional interactions between inferotemporal and prefrontal cortex in a cognitive task. *Brain Research, 330*, 299-307.

Gaffan, D. (1972). Loss of recognition memory in rats with lesions of the fornix. *Neuropsychologia, 10*, 327-341.

Gaffan, D. (1974). Recognition impaired and association intact in the memory of monkeys after transection of the fornix. *Journal of Comparative and Physiological Psychology, 86*, 1100-1109.

Gaffan, D., & Harrison, S. (1987). Amygdalectomy and disconnection in visual learning for auditory secondary reinforcement by monkeys. *Journal of Neuroscience, 7*, 2285-2292.

Gallistel, C. R., Shizgal, P., & Yeomans, J. S. (1981). A portrait of the substrate for self-stimulation. *Psychological Review, 88*, 228-273.

Gentilini, M., de Renzi, E., & Crisi, G. (1987). Bilateral paramedian thalamic artery infarcts: Report of eight cases. *Journal of Neurology, Neurosurgery and Psychiatry, 50*, 900-909.

Gerfen, C. R. (1992). The neostriatal mosaic: Multiple levels of compartmental organization in the basal ganglia. *Annual Review of Neuroscience, 15*, 285-320.

Glees, P., & Griffeth, H. B. (1952). Bilateral destruction of the hippocampus (*Cornu Ammonis*) in a case of dementia. *Monatsschrift für Psychiatrie und Neurologie, 123*, 193-204.

Glickman, S. E., & Schiff, B. B. (1967). A biological theory of reinforcement. *Psychological Review, 74*, 81-109.

Gloor, P. (1960). Amygdala. In J. Field. (Ed.), *Handbook of Physiology, Section 1: Neurophysiology.* Vol. 2. (pp. 1395-1420). Washington, DC: American Physiological Society.

Gloor, P., Olivier, A., Quesney, L. F., Andermann, F., & Horowitz, S. (1982). The role of the limbic system in experiential phenomena of temporal lobe epilepsy. *Annals of Neurology, 12*, 129-144.

Gold, L. H., Swerdlow, N. R., & Koob, G. F. (1988). The role of mesolimbic dopamine in conditioned locomotion produced by amphetamine. *Behavioral Neuroscience, 102*, 544-552.

Goldman-Racic, P. S. (1988). Topography of cognition: Parallel distributed networks in primate association cortex. *Annual Review of Neuroscience, 11*, 137-156.

Gollin, E. S. (1960). Developmental studies of visual recognition of incomplete objects. *Perceptual and Motor Skills, 11*, 289-298.

Goltsev, A. (1996). An assembly neural network for texture segmentation. *Neural Networks, 9*, 643-653.

Goodale, M. A., & Milner, A. D. (1992). Separate visual pathways for perception and action. *Trends in Neurosciences, 15*, 20-25.

Goodale, M. A., Milner, A. D., Jakobson, L. S., & Carey, D. P. (1991). A neurological dissociation between perceiving objects and grasping them. *Nature, 349*, 154-156.

Graff-Radford, N. R., Tranel, D., Van Hoesen, G. W., & Brandt, J. P. (1990). Diencephalic amnesia. *Brain, 113*, 1-25.

Gray, C. M., König, P., Engel, A. K., & Singer, W. (1989). Oscillatory responses in cat visual cortex exhibit inter-columnar synchronization which reflects global stimulus properties. *Nature, 338*, 334-337.

Gray, C. M., & McCormick, D. A. (1996). Chattering cells: Superficial pyramidal neurons contributing to the generation of synchronous oscillations in the visual cortex. *Science, 274*, 109-113.

Gray, C. M., & Singer, W. (1989). Stimulus-specific neuronal oscillations in orientation columns of cat visual cortex. *Proceedings of the National Academy of Sciences U.S.A., 86*, 1698-1702.

Graybiel, A. M. (1990). Neurotransmitters and neuromodulators in the basal ganglia. *Trends in Neurosciences, 13*, 244-254.

Graybiel, A. M., & Ragsdale, C. W. (1978). Histochemically distinct compartments in the striatum of human being, monkey and cat demonstrated by the acetylthiocholinesterase staining method. *Proceedings of the National Academy of Sciences U.S.A., 75*, 5723-5726.

Graybiel, A. M., & Ragsdale Jr., C. W. (1983). Biochemical anatomy of the striatum. In P. C. Emion. (Ed.), *Chemical Neuroanatomy.* (pp. 427-504). New York: Raven Press.

Green, R. H., Beatty, W. W., & Schwartzbaum, J. S. (1967). Comparative effects of septo-hippocampal and caudate lesions on avoidance behavior in rats. *Journal of Comparative and Physiological Psychology, 64*, 444-452.

Grillner, S., Wallén, P., Brodin, L., & Lansner, A. (1991). Neuronal network generating locomotor behavior in lamprey: Circuitry, transmitters, membrane properties, and simulation. *Annual Review of Neuroscience, 14*, 169-199.

Gross, C. G., Bender, D. B., & Rocha-Miranda, C. E. (1969). Visual receptive fields of neurons in inferotemporal cortex of the monkey. *Science, 166*, 1303-1306.

Grossberg, S. (1975). A neural model of attention, reinforcement, and discrimination learning. *International Review of Neurobiology, 18*, 263-327.

Grossberg, S., & Levine, D. S. (1987). Neural dynamics of attentionally modulated Pavlovian conditioning: Blocking, interstimulus interval, and secondary reinforcement. *Applied Optics, 26*, 5015-5030.

Hartley, D. (1959). *Various conjectures on the perception, motion, and generation of ideas (1746).* Los Angeles: The Augustan Reprint Society.

Hebb, D. O. (1949). *The Organization of Behavior.* New York: Wiley.

Hebb, D. O. (1980). *Essay on mind.* Hillsdale, NJ: Lawrence Erlbaum Associates.

Hildebrand, J. G., & Shepherd, G. M. (1997). Mechanisms of olfactory discrimination: Converging evidence for common principles across phyla. *Annual Review of Neuroscience, 20*, 595-631.

Hinsey, J. C. (1940). The hypothalamus and somatic responses. *Research Publications of the Association for Research in Nervous and Mental Disease, 20*, 657-685.

Hiroi, N., & White, N. M. (1991). The lateral nucleus of the amygdala mediates expression of the amphetamine conditioned place preference. *Journal of Neuroscience, 11*, 2107-2116.

Hirsh, R. (1974). The hippocampus and contextual retrieval of information from memory: A theory. *Behavioral Biology, 12*, 421-444.

Hirsh, R. (1980). The hippocampus, conditional operations, and cognition. *Physiological Psychology, 8*, 175-182.

Hoffmann, K. P., & Stone, J. (1971). Conduction velocity of afferents to cat visual cortex: A correlation with cortical receptive field properties. *Brain Research, 32*, 460-466.

Hopfield, J. J., & Tank, D. W. (1986). Computing with neural circuits: A model. *Science, 233*, 625-633.

Hopfield, J. J., & Tank, D. W. (1989). Neural architecture and biophysics for sequence recognition. In J. H. Byrne & W. O. Berry. (Eds.), *Neural models of plasticity*. (pp. 363-377). San Diego: Academic Press.

Hornykiewicz, O. (1966). Dopamine (3-hydroxytyramine) and brain function. *Pharmacological Review, 18*, 925-964.

Hubel, D. H., & Wiesel, T. N. (1959). Receptive fields of single neurones in the cat's striate cortex. *Journal of Physiology (London), 148*, 574-591.

Hudson, B. B. (1950). One-trial learning in the domestic rat. *Genetic Psychology Monographs, 41*, 99-145.

Hume, D. (1777/1946). *Enquiries concerning the human understanding*. Oxford: Clarendon Press.

Hummel, J. E., & Biederman, I. (1992). Dynamic binding in a neural network for shape recognition. *Psychological Review, 99*, 480-517.

Isaac, W., & De Vito, J. L. (1958). Effect of sensory stimulation on the activity of normal and prefrontal-lobectomized monkeys. *Journal of Comparative and Physiological Psychology, 51*, 172-174.

Ishai, A., Ungerleider, L. G., Martin, A., Maisog, J. M., & Haxby, J. V. (1997). fMRI reveals differential activation in the ventral vision pathway during the perception of different object categories. *Society for Neuroscience Abstracts, 23*, 2229.

Jacoby, L. L., & Witherspoon, D. (1982). Remembering without awareness. *Canadian Journal of Psychology, 36*, 300-324.

James, W. (1890). *The Principles of Psychology*. New York: Henry Holt.

Jenkins, H. M., & Moore, B. R. (1973). The form of the auto-shaped response with food or water reinforcers. *Journal of the Experimental Analysis of Behavior, 20*, 163-181.

Jiménez-Castellanos, J., & Graybiel, A. M. (1989). Compartmental origins of striatal efferent projections in the cat. *Neuroscience, 32*, 297-321.

Jones, E. G. (1974). The anatomy of the extrageniculostriate visual mechanisms. In F. O. Schmitt & F. G. Worden. (Eds.), *The neurosciences: Third study program*. (pp. 215-227). Cambridge, MA: MIT Press.

Kaada, B. R. (1951). Somato-motor, autonomic and electrocorticographic responses to electrical stimulation of "rhinencephalic" and other structures in primate, cat and dog. *Acta Physiologica Scandinavica, 24*, Suppl. 83, 1-285.

Kamin, L. J. (1969). Predictability, surprise, attention and conditioning. In B. A. Campbell & R. M. Church. (Eds.), *Punishment and aversive behavior*. (pp. 279-296). New York: Appleton-Century-Crofts.

Kanwisher, N., McDermott, J., & Chun, M. M. (1997). The fusiform face area: A module in human extrastriate cortex specialized for face perception. *Journal of Neuroscience, 17*, 4302-4311.

Kanwisher, N., Weinrib, O., Tong, F., & Nakayama, K. (1997). Responses of the human fusiform face area to facelike stimuli. *Society for Neuroscience Abstracts, 23*, 2229.

Kaplan, S., Sonntag, M., & Chown, E. (1991). Tracing recurrent activity in cognitive elements (TRACE): A model of temporal dynamics in a cell assembly. *Connection Science, 3*, 179-206.

Kauer, J. S. (1991). Contributions of topography and parallel processing to odor coding in the vertebrate olfactory pathway. *Trends in Neurosciences, 14*, 79-85.

Kaye, K. L., & Bower, T. G. R. (1994). Learning and intermodal transfer of information in newborns. *Psychological Science, 5*, 286-288.

Kimura, M., Rajkowski, J., & Evarts, E. (1984). Tonically discharging putamen neurons exhibit set-dependent responses. *Proceedings of the National Academy of Sciences U.S.A., 81*, 4998-5001.

Klüver, H., & Bucy, P. C. (1938). An analysis of certain effects of bilateral temporal lobectomy in the rhesus monkey with special reference to "psychic blindness." *Journal of Psychology, 5*, 33-54.

Klüver, H., & Bucy, P. C. (1939). Preliminary analysis of functions of the temporal lobe in monkeys. *Archives of Neurology and Psychiatry, 42*, 979-1000.

Knight, D. E., von Grafenstein, H., & Athayde, C. M. (1989). Calcium-dependent and calcium-independent exocytosis. *Trends in Neurosciences, 11*, 451-458.

Köhler, W., & Wallach, H. (1944). Figural after-effects: an investigation of visual processes. *Proceedings of the American Philosophical Society, 88*, 269-357.

König, P., Engel, A. K., & Singer, W. (1996). Integrator or coincidence detector? The role of the cortical neuron revisited. *Trends in Neurosciences, 19*, 130-137.

Korsakoff, S. S. (1889). Etude médico-psychologique sur une forme des maladies de la mémoire. *Revue de Philosophie, 28*, 501-530.

Kreiter, A. K., & Singer, W. (1996). Stimulus-dependent synchronization of neuronal responses in the visual cortex of the awake macaque monkey. *Journal of Neuroscience, 16*, 2381-2396.

Külpe, O. (1901). *Outlines of psychology*. London: Swan Sonnenschein.

Kurumiya, S., & Nakajima, S. (1988). Dopamine D1 receptors in the nucleus accumbens: Involvement in the reinforcing effect of tegmental stimulation. *Brain Research, 448*, 1-6.

Lashley, K. S. (1924). Studies of cerebral function in learning. VI. The theory that synaptic resistance is reduced by the passage of a nerve impulse. *Psychological Review, 31*, 369-375.

Lashley, K. S. (1929). *Brain mechanisms and intelligence*. Chicago: University of Chicago Press.

Lashley, K. S. (1938). Experimental analysis of instinctive behavior. *Psychological Review, 45*, 445-471.

Lashley, K. S. (1942). The problem of cerebral organization in vision. In H. Klüver. (Ed.), *Visual mechanisms. Biological symposia*, Vol. 7. (pp. 301-322). Lancaster, PA: Cattell Press.

Lashley, K. S. (1947). Structural variation in the nervous system in relation to behavior. *Psychological Review, 54*, 325-334.

Lashley, K. S. (1950). In search of the engram. *Symposia of the Society for Experimental Biology, 4*, 454-482.

Lashley, K. S. (1951). The problem of serial order in behavior. In L. A. Jeffress. (Ed.), *Cerebral mechanisms in behavior*. (pp. 112-136). New York: Wiley.

Leão, A. A. P. (1944). Spreading depression of activity in the cerebral cortex. *Journal of Neurophysiology, 7*, 359-390.

Leaton, R. N. (1965). Exploration behavior in rats with hippocampal lesions. *Journal of Comparative and Physiological Psychology, 59*, 325-330.

Lee-Teng, E. (1969). Retrograde amnesia in relation to subconvulsive and convulsive currents in chicks. *Journal of Comparative and Physiological Psychology, 67*, 135-139.

Leri, F., & Franklin, K. B. J. (1996). Learning deficits induced by pontine tegmentum lesions: Artifact of anxiety. *Society for Neuroscience Abstracts, 22*, 146.

Lewicki, M. S., & Konishi, M. (1995). Mechanisms underlying the sensitivity of songbird forebrain neurons to temporal order. *Proceedings of the National Academy of Sciences U.S.A., 92*, 5582-5586.

Li, Z. (1994). Modeling the sensory computations of the olfactory bulb. In E. Domany, J. L. van Hemmen, & K. Schulten. (Eds.), *Models of neural networks II*. (pp. 221-251). New York: Springer-Verlag.

Llinas, R., & Ribary, U. (1993). Coherent 40-Hz oscillation characterizes dream state in humans. *Proceedings of the National Academy of Sciences U.S.A., 90*, 2078-2081.

Locke, J. (1700/1959). *An essay concerning human understanding*. New York: Dover Publications.

Lorente de Nó, R. (1938). Analysis of the activity of the chains of internuncial neurons. *Journal of Neurophysiology, 1*, 207-244.

MacCorquodale, K., & Meehl, P. E. (1954). Edward C. Tolman. In A. T. Poffenberger. (Ed.), *Modern Learning Theory*. (pp. 177-266). New York: Appleton, Century, Crofts.

Mackintosh, N. J. (1975). A theory of attention: Variations in the associability of stimuli with reinforcement. *Psychological Review, 82,* 276-298.

Magendie, F. (1841). *Leçons sur les fonctions et les maladies du système nerveux.* Paris:

Marshall, J. F., & Teitelbaum, P. (1977). New considerations in the neurophysiology of motivated behaviors. In L. L. Iversen, S. D. Iversen, & S. H. Snyder. (Eds.), *Handbook of psychopharmacology.* Vol 7. (pp. 201-229). New York: Plenum Press.

Mattingly, B. A., Gotsick, J. E., & Salamanca, K. (1988). Latent sensitization to apomorphine following repeated low doses. *Behavioral Neuroscience, 102,* 553-558.

Maunsell, J. H. R. (1995). The brain's visual world: Representation of visual targets in cerebral cortex. *Science, 270,* 764-768.

McCormick, D. A., & Thompson, R. F. (1984). Cerebellum: Essential involvement in the classically conditioned eyelid response. *Science, 223,* 296-299.

McDonald, R. J., & White, N. M. (1993). A triple dissociation of memory systems: Hippocampus, amygdala, and dorsal striatum. *Behavioral Neuroscience, 107,* 3-22.

Meberg, P. J., Barnes, C. A., McNaughton, B. L., & Routtenberg, A. (1993). Protein kinase C and F1/GAP-43 gene expression in hippocampus inversely related to synaptic enhancement lasting 3 days. *Proceedings of the National Academy of Sciences U.S.A., 90,* 12050-12054.

Meltzoff, A. N., & Moore, K. M. (1989). Imitation in newborn infants: Exploring the range of gestures imitated and the underlying mechanisms. *Developmental Psychology, 25,* 954-962.

Mesulam, M.- M. (1983). The functional anatomy and hemispheric specialization for directed attention. *Trends in Neurosciences, 6,* 384-387.

Mettler, F. A., & Mettler, C. C. (1942). The effects of striatal injury. *Brain, 65,* 242-255.

Miliaressis, E., Malette, J., & Coulombe, D. (1986). The effects of pimozide on the reinforcing efficacy of central grey stimulation in the rat. *Behavioral Brain Research, 21,* 95-100.

Miller, R. R., & Marlin, N. A. (1984). The physiology and semantics of consolidation. In H. Weingartner & E. S. Parker. (Eds.), *Memory consolidation.* (pp. 85-110). Hillsdale, NJ: Lawrence Erlbaum Associates.

Miller, R., & Wickens, J. R. (1991). Corticostriatal cell assemblies in selective attention and in representation of predictable and controllable events. A general statement of corticostriatal interplay and the role of striatal dopamine. *Concepts in neuroscience, 2,* 65-94.

Milner, B. (1959). The memory defect in bilateral hippocampal lesions. *Psychiatric Research Reports, 11,* 43-52.

Milner, B. (1962). Les troubles de la mémoire accompagnant des lésions hippocampiques bilatérales. In *Physiologie de l'hippocampe.* (pp. 257-270). Paris: Editions C.N.R.S..

Milner, B. (1968). Visual recognition and recall after right temporal-lobe excision in man. *Neuropsychologia, 6,* 191-209.

Milner, B. (1970). Pathologie de la mémoire. In *La mémoire: Symposium de l'association de psychologie scientifique de langue française.* (pp. 185-212). Vendôme: Presses Universitaires de France.

Milner, B., Corkin, S., & Teuber, H.- L. (1968). Further analysis of the hippocampal amnesic syndrome: 14-year follow-up study of H.M. *Neuropsychologia, 6,* 215-234.

Milner, B., Squire, L. R., & Kandel, E. R. (1998). Cognitive neuroscience and the study of memory. *Neuron, 20,* 445-468.

Milner, P. M. (1957). The cell assembly: Mk. II. *Psychological Review, 64,* 242-252.

Milner, P. M. (1960). Learning in neural systems. In M. C. Yovits & S. Cameron. (Eds.), *Self-organizing systems.* (pp. 190-204). New York: Pergamon Press.

Milner, P. M. (1961a). A neural mechanism for the immediate recall of sequences. *Kybernetik, 1,* 76-81.

Milner, P. M. (1961b). The application of physiology to learning theory. In R. A. Patton. (Ed.), *Current trends in psychological theory.* (pp. 111-133). Pittsburgh, PA: University of Pittsburgh Press.

Milner, P. M. (1970). *Physiological psychology.* New York: Holt, Rinehart & Winston, Inc..

Milner, P. M. (1974). A model for visual shape recognition. *Psychological Review, 81*, 521-535.

Milner, P. M. (1976). Models of motivation and reinforcement. In A. Wauquier & E. T. Rolls. (Eds.), *Brain-stimulation reward.* (pp. 543-556). Amsterdam: North-Holland.

Milner, P. M. (1989). A cell assembly theory of hippocampal amnesia. *Neuropsychologia, 27*, 23-30.

Milner, P. M. (1991). Brain-stimulation reward: A review. *Canadian Journal of Psychology, 45*, 1-36.

Milner, P. M. (1996). Neural representations: Some old problems revisited. *Journal of Cognitive Neuroscience, 8*, 69-77.

Mishkin, M. (1982). A memory system in the monkey. *Philosophical Transactions of the Royal Society of London B, 298*, 85-95.

Mishkin, M. (1993). Cerebral memory circuits. In T. A. Poggio & D. A. Glaser. (Eds.), *Exploring brain function: Models in neuroscience.* (pp. 113-125). New York: Wiley.

Mishkin, M., & Appenzeller, T. (1987). The anatomy of memory. *Scientific American, 256* (6), 80-90.

Mishkin, M., Malamut, B., & Bachevalier, J. (1984). Memories and habits: Two neural systems. In G. Lynch, J. L. McGaugh, & N. M. Weinberger. (Eds.), *Neurobiology of learning and memory.* (pp. 65-77). New York: Guilford Press.

Mishkin, M., & Petri, H. L. (1984). Memories and habits: Some implications for the analysis of learning and retention. In L. R. Squire & N. Butters. (Eds.), *Neuropsychology of memory.* (pp. 287-296). New York: Guilford Press.

Miyashita, Y. (1993). Inferior temporal cortex: Where visual perception meets memory. *Annual Review of Neuroscience, 16*, 245-263.

Mogenson, G. J., Jones, D. L., & Yim, C. Y. (1980). From motivation to action: Functional interface between the limbic system and the motor system. *Progress in Neurobiology, 14*, 69-97.

Mogenson, G. J., Takigawa, M., Robertson, A., & Wu, M. (1979). Self-stimulation of the nucleus accumbens and ventral tegmental area of Tsai attenuated by microinjections of spiroperidol into the nucleus accumbens. *Brain Research, 171*, 247-259.

Mora, F., Sanguinetti, A. M., Rolls, E. T., & Shaw, S. G. (1975). Differential effects on self-stimulation and motor behaviour produced by microintracranial injections of a dopamine-receptor blocking agent. *Neuroscience Letters, 1*, 179-184.

Moran, J., & Desimone, R. (1985). Selective attention gates visual processing in the extrastriate cortex. *Science, 229*, 782-784.

Moruzzi, G., & Magoun, H. W. (1949). Brain stem reticular formation and activation of the EEG. *Electroencephalography and Clinical Neurophysiology, 1*, 455-473.

Moscovitch, M. (1995). Recovered consciousness: A hypothesis concerning modularity and episodic memory. *Journal of clinical and experimental neuropsychology, 17*, 276-290.

Moscovitch, M., Goshen-Gottstein, Y., & Vriezen, E. (1994). Memory without conscious recollection: A tutorial review from a neuropsychological perspective. In C. Umiltà & M. Moscovitch. (Eds.), *Attention and performance XV: Conscious and nonconscious information processing.* (pp. 619-660). Cambridge, MA: MIT Press.

Müller, G. E., & Pilzecker, A. (1900). Experimentelle Beiträge zur Lehre vom Gedächtniss. *Zeitschrift fur Psychologie und Physiologie der Sinnesorgane, Erganzungsband 1*, 1-288.

Nadel, L., & Moscovitch, M. (1997). Memory consolidation, retrograde amnesia and the hippocampal complex. *Current Opinion in Neurobiology, 7*, 217-227.

Nakajima, S. (1986). Suppression of operant responding in the rat by dopamine D1 receptor blockade with SCH 23390. *Physiological Psychology, 14*, 111-114.

Nakajima, S. (1988). Involvement of dopamine D2 receptors in the reinforcement of operant behavior. *Society for Neuroscience Abstracts, 14*, 1101.

Nakajima, S. (1989). Subtypes of dopamine receptors involved in the mechanism of reinforcement. *Neuroscience and Biobehavioral Review, 13*, 123-128.

Nakajima, S., & Baker, J. D. (1989). Effects of D2 dopamine receptor blockade with raclopride on intracranial self-stimulation and food-reinforced operant behaviour. *Psychopharmacology*, *98*, 330-333.

O'Keefe, J., & Dostrovsky, J. (1971). The hippocampus as a cognitive map. Preliminary evidence from unit activity in freely moving rat. *Brain Research*, *34*, 171-175.

O'Keefe, J., & Nadel, L. (1978). *The hippocampus as a cognitive map*. Oxford: Clarendon Press.

Olds, J. (1976). Reward and drive neurons: 1975. In A. Wauquier & E. T. Rolls. (Eds.), *Brain-stimulation reward*. (pp. 1-27). Amsterdam: North-Holland.

Olds, J., Killam, K. F., & Bach-y-Rita, P. (1956). Self-stimulation of the brain used as a screening method for tranquilizing drugs. *Science*, *124*, 265-266.

Olds, J., & Milner, P. M. (1954). Positive reinforcement produced by electrical stimulation of septal area and other regions of rat brain. *Journal of Comparative and Physiological Psychology*, *47*, 419-427.

Olds, J., & Olds, M. E. (1965). Drives, rewards, and the brain. In T. M. Newcomb. (Ed.), *New directions in psychology*. Vol 2. (pp. 327-410). New York: Holt, Rinehart & Winston.

Olds, J., & Travis, R. P. (1960). Effects of chlorpromazine, meprobamate, pentobarbital and morphine on self-stimulation. *Journal of Pharmacology and Experimental Therapeutics*, *128*, 397-404.

Olds, M. E., & Olds, J. (1963). Approach-avoidance analysis of rat diencephalon. *Journal of Comparative Neurology*, *120*, 259-295.

Olton, D. S., Becker, J. T., & Handelmann, G. E. (1979). Hippocampus, space, and memory. *Behavioral and Brain Sciences*, *2*, 313-365.

Orbach, J., Milner, B., & Rasmussen, T. (1960). Learning and retention in monkeys after amygdala-hippocampus resection. *Archives of Neurology*, *3*, 230-251.

Otto, T., Schottler, F., Staubli, U., Eichenbaum, H., & Lynch, G. (1991). Hippocampus and olfactory discrimination learning: Effects of entorhinal cortex lesions on olfactory learning and memory in a successive-cue, go--no-go task. *Behavioral Neuroscience*, *105*, 111-119.

Packard, M. G., Hirsh, R., & White, N. M. (1989). Differential effects of fornix and caudate nucleus lesions on two radial maze tasks: Evidence for multiple memory systems. *Journal of Neuroscience*, *9*, 1465-1472.

Packard, M. G., & White, N. M. (1989). Memory facilitation produced by dopamine agonists: Role of receptor subtype and mnemonic requirements. *Pharmacology Biochemistry and Behavior*, *33*, 511-518.

Palm, G. (1982). *Neural assemblies. An alternative approach to artificial intelligence*. Berlin: Springer-Verlag.

Pampiglione, G., & Falconer, M. A. (1960). Electrical stimulation of the hippocampus in man. In J. Field, H. W. Magoun, & V. E. Hall. (Eds.), *Handbook of physiology, II*. (pp. 1391-1394). Washington, DC: American Physiological Society.

Pan, H. S., Penney, J. B., & Young, A. B. (1985). Γ-aminobutyric acid and benzodiazepine receptor changes induced by unilateral 6-hydroxydopamine lesions of the medial forebrain bundle. *Journal of Neurochemistry*, *45*, 1396-1404.

Parent, A. (1990). Extrinsic connections of the basal ganglia. *Trends in Neurosciences*, *13*, 254-258.

Pavlov, I. P. (1927). *Conditioned reflexes: An investigation of the physiological activity of the cerebral cortex*. New York: Dover.

Penfield, W., & Jasper, H. (1954). *Epilepsy and the functional anatomy of the human brain*. Boston: Little, Brown.

Penfield, W., & Milner, B. (1958). Memory deficit produced by bilateral lesions in the hippocampal zone. *AMA Archives of Neurology and Psychiatry*, *79*, 475-497.

Penfield, W., & Perot, P. (1963). The brain's record of auditory and visual experience. *Brain*, *86*, 595-696.

Penfield, W., & Roberts, L. (1959). *Speech and brain mechanisms*. Princeton, NJ: Princeton University Press.

Perrett, D. I., Oram, M. W., Harries, M. H., Bevan, R., Hietanen, J. K., Benson, P. J., & Thomas, S. (1991). Viewer-centred and object-centred coding of heads in the macaque temporal cortex. *Experimental Brain Research, 86*, 159-173.

Perrett, D. I., Rolls, E. T., & Caan, W. (1982). Visual neurons responsive to faces in the monkey temporal cortex. *Experimental Brain Research, 47*, 329-342.

Petitto, L. A., & Marentette, P. F. (1991). Babbling in the manual mode: Evidence for the ontogeny of language. *Science, 251*, 1493-1496.

Petitto, L. A., Zatorre, R. J., Nikelski, E. J., Gauna, K., Dostie, D., & Evans, A. C. (1997). Cerebral organization for language in the absence of sound: A PET study of deaf signers processing signed languages. *Society for Neuroscience Abstracts, 23*, 2228.

Phillips, A. G., Blaha, C. D., & Fibiger, H. C. (1989). Neurochemical correlates of brain-stimulation reward measured by ex vivo and in vivo analyses. *Neuroscience and Biobehavioral Review, 13*, 99-104.

Podhorna, J., & Franklin, K. B. J. (1998). Lesions of the pedunculopontine nucleus increase anxiety in rats. *NeuroReport, 9*, 1783-1786.

Polster, M. R., Nadel, L., & Schacter, D. L. (1991). Cognitive neuroscience analyses of memory: A historical perspective. *Journal of Cognitive Neuroscience, 3*, 95-116.

Pulvermüller, F. (1999). Words in the brain's language. *Behavioral and Brain Sciences, 22*, 253-336.

Randrup, A., Munkvad, I., & Udsen, P. (1963). Adrenergic mechanisms and amphetamine induced abnormal behavior. *Acta Pharmacologia et Toxicologia, 20*, 145-157.

Ranson, S. W., & Magoun, H. W. (1933). Respiratory and pupillary reactions induced by electrical stimulation of the hypothalamus. *Archives of Neurology and Psychiatry, 29*, 1179-1193.

Rescorla, R. A., & Wagner, A. R. (1972). A theory of Pavlovian conditioning: Variations in the effectiveness of reinforcement and nonreinforcement. In A. H. Black & W. F. Prokasy. (Eds.), *Classical conditioning II.* (pp. 64-99). New York: Appleton-Century-Crofts.

Ribot, T. (1892). Memory. In D. H. Tuke. (Ed.), *A dictionary of psychological medicine.* (pp. 798-801). Philadelphia: Blakiston.

Richter, C. P., & Hines, M. (1938). Increased spontaneous activity produced in monkeys by brain lesions. *Brain, 61*, 1-16.

Riedel, G., Harrington, N. R., Hall, G., & Macphail, E. M. (1997). Nucleus accumbens lesions impair context, but not cue, conditioning in rats. *NeuroReport, 8*, 2477-2481.

Riesen, A. H. (1947). The development of visual perception in man and chimpanzee. *Science, 106*, 107-108.

Ringo, J. L., Doty, R. W., Demeter, S., & Simard, P. Y. (1994). Time is of the essence: A conjecture that hemispheric specialization arises from interhemispheric conduction delay. *Cerebral Cortex, 4*, 331-343.

Rioch, D. McK., & Brenner, C. (1938). Experiments on the corpus striatum and rhinencephalon. *Journal of Comparative Neurology, 68*, 491-507.

Rizzolatti, G. (1983). Mechanisms of selective attention in mammals. In J.- P. Ewert, R. R. Capranica, & D. J. Ingle. (Eds.), *Advances in vertebrate neuroethology.* (pp. 261-297). New York: Plenum.

Rizzolatti, G., & Arbib, M. A. (1998). Language within our grasp. *Trends in Neurosciences, 21*, 188-194.

Rizzolatti, G., Riggio, L., & Sheliga, B. M. (1994). Space and selective attention. In C. Umiltà & M. Moscovitch. (Eds.), *Attention and performance XV.* (pp. 231-265). Cambridge, MA: MIT Press.

Robbins, T. W. (1976). Relationship between reward-enhancing and stereotypical effects of psychomotor stimulant drugs. *Nature, 264*, 57-59.

Robbins, T. W., Cador, M., Taylor, J. R., & Everitt, B. J. (1989). Limbic-striatal interactions in reward-related processes. *Neuroscience and Biobehavioral Review, 13*, 155-162.

Roberts, W. W., Dember, W. N., & Brodwick, M. (1962). Alternation and exploration in rats with hippocampal lesions. *Journal of Comparative and Physiological Psychology, 55*, 695-700.

Roelfsema, P. R., Engel, A. K., König, P., & Singer, W. (1997). Visuomotor integration is associated with zero time-lag synchronization among cortical areas. *Nature*, *385*, 157-161.

Rompré, P.- P., & Shizgal, P. (1986). Electrophysiological characteristics of neurons in forebrain regions implicated in self-stimulation of the medial forebrain bundle in the rat. *Brain Research*, *364*, 338-349.

Rompré, P.- P., & Wise, R. A. (1989). Opiod-neuroleptic interaction in brainstem self-stimulation. *Brain Research*, *477*, 144-151.

Rosenblatt, F. (1962). *Principles of neurodynamics: Perceptrons and the theory of brain mechanisms*. Washington, DC: Spartan Books.

Rosene, D. L., & Van Hoesen, G. W. (1977). Hippocampal efferents reach widespread areas of cerebral cortex and amygdala in the rhesus monkey. *Science*, *198*, 315-317.

Rosvold, H. E., Mirsky, A. F., & Pribram, K. H. (1954). Influence of amygdalectomy on social behavior in monkeys. *Journal of Comparative and Physiological Psychology*, *47*, 173-178.

Routtenberg, A. (1985). Commentary. Protein kinase C activation leading to protein F1 phosphorylation may regulate synaptic plasticity by presynaptic terminal growth. *Behavioral and Neural Biology*, *44*, 186-200.

Routtenberg, A. (1986). Synaptic plasticity and protein kinase C. *Progress in brain research*, *69*, 211-234.

Ruch, T. C., & Shenkin, H. A. (1943). The relation of area 13 on orbital surface of frontal lobes to hyperactivity and hyperphagia in monkeys. *Journal of Neurophysiology*, *6*, 349-360.

Rumelhart, D. E., & McClelland, J. L. (1986). *Parallel distributed processing, volume 1: Foundations*. Cambridge, MA: MIT Press.

Russell, W. R., & Nathan, P. W. (1946). Traumatic amnesia. *Brain*, *69*, 280-300.

Sakata, H., Taira, M., Kusunoki, M., Murata, A., & Tanaka, Y. (1997). The parietal association cortex in depth perception and visual control of hand action. *Trends in Neurosciences*, *20*, 350-357.

Scarborough, D. L., Cortese, C., & Scarborough, H. (1977). Frequency and repetition effects in lexical memory. *Journal of Experimental Psychology: Human Perception and Performance*, *3*, 1-17.

Schacter, D. L. (1987). Memory, amnesia and frontal lobe dysfunction. *Psychobiology*, *15*, 21-36.

Schacter, D. L. (1992). Semon, Richard. In L. R. Squire. (Ed.), *Encyclopedia of learning and memory*. (pp. 586-588). New York: Macmillan.

Schacter, D. L. (1994). Implicit memory in amnesic patients: Evidence for spared auditory priming. *Psychological Science*, *5*, 20-25.

Scoville, W. B., & Milner, B. (1957). Loss of recent memory after bilateral hippocampal lesions. *Journal of Neurology, Neurosurgery and Psychiatry*, *20*, 11-21.

Sechenov, I. M. (1965). *Reflexes of the brain*. Cambridge, MA: M.I.T. Press. (Original published 1863)

Semon, R. W. (1921). *The mneme*. London: Allen and Unwin.

Shepherd, G. M. (1987). The olfactory bulb. In G. Adelman. (Ed.), *Encyclopedia of neuroscience* Vol. II, (pp. 879-881). Boston: Birkhäuser.

Sidman, M., Stoddard, L. T., & Mohr, J. P. (1968). Some additional quantitative observations of immediate memory in a patient with bilateral hippocampal lesions. *Neuropsychologia*, *6*, 245-254.

Singer, W. (1994). Coherence as an organizing principle of cortical functions. *International Review of Neurobiology*, *37*, 153-183.

Singer, W., & Gray, C. M. (1995). Visual feature integration and the temporal correlation hypothesis. *Annual Review of Neuroscience*, *18*, 555-586.

Skinner, B. F., & Heron, W. T. (1937). Effects of caffeine and benzedrine upon conditioning and extinction. *Psychological Record*, *1*, 340-346.

Smith, A. D., & Bolam, J. P. (1990). The neural network of the basal ganglia as revealed by the study of synaptic connections of identified neurones. *Trends in Neurosciences*, *13*, 259-265.

Sperry, R. W. (1952). Neurology and the mind-brain problem. *American Scientist, 40*, 291-312.

Squire, L. R. (1987). Memory: Neural organization and behavior. In F. Plum. (Ed.), *Handbook of physiology: Higher functions of the brain, V: Section I. The nervous system.* (4th ed., pp. 295-371). Bethesda, MD: American Physiological Society.

Squire, L. R., & Cohen, N. (1979). Memory and amnesia: Resistance to disruption develops for years after learning. *Behavioral and Neural Biology, 25*, 115-125.

Squire, L. R., & Cohen, N. J. (1982). Remote memory, retrograde amnesia, and the neuropsychology of memory. In L. S. Cermak. (Ed.), *Human memory and amnesia.* (pp. 275-303). Hillsdale, NJ: Lawrence Erlbaum Associates.

Squire, L. R., Slater, P. C., & Chace, P. M. (1975). Retrograde amnesia: Temporal gradient in very long term memory following electroconvulsive therapy. *Science, 187*, 77-79.

Squire, L. R., & Zola-Morgan, S. (1991). The medial temporal lobe memory system. *Science, 253*, 1380-1386.

Squire, L. R., Zola-Morgan, S., & Alvarez, P. (1994). Functional distinctions within the medial temporal lobe memory system: What is the evidence? *Behavioral and Brain Sciences, 17*, 495-496.

Starr, A., & Phillips, L. (1970). Verbal and motor memory in the amnestic syndrome. *Neuropsychologia, 8*, 75-88.

Stellar, J. R. & Corbett, D. (1989). Regional neuroleptic Micro injections indicate a role for nucleus accumbens in lateral hypothalamic self-stimulation reward. *Brain Research, 477*, 126-143.

Stellar, J. R., Kelley, A. E., & Corbett, D. (1983). Effects of peripheral and central dopamine blockade on lateral hypothalamic self-stimulation: Evidence for both reward and motor deficits. *Pharmacology Biochemistry and Behavior, 18*, 433-442.

Stent, G. S., Kristan, W. B. Jr., Friesen, W. O., Ort, C. A., Poon, M., & Calabrese, R. L. (1978). Neuronal generation of the leech swimming movement. *Science, 200*, 1348-1357.

Strupp, M., Brüning, R., Wu, R. H., Deimling, M., Reiser, M., & Brandt, T. (1998). Diffusion-weighted MRI in transient global amnesia: Elevated signal intensity in the left mesial temporal lobe in 7 of 10 patients. *Annals of Neurology, 43*, 164-170.

Suzuki, W. A., Fiorani Jr., M., & Desimone, R. (1997). Location and scene selective responses in the macaque entorhinal and perirhinal cortices. *Society for Neuroscience Abstracts, 23*, 2230.

Székely, G. (1968). Development of limb movements: Embryological, physiological, and model studies. In G. E. W. Wolstenholme & M. O'Connor. (Eds.), *CIBA foundation symposium on growth of nervous system.* (pp. 77-93). London: Churchill Press.

Tanaka, K. (1992). Inferotemporal cortex and higher visual functions. *Current Opinion in Neurobiology, 2*, 502-505.

Teitelbaum, H., & Milner, P. M. (1963). Activity changes following partial hippocampal lesions in rats. *Journal of Comparative and Physiological Psychology, 56*, 284-289.

Teyler, T. J., & DiScenna, P. (1986). The hippocampal memory indexing theory. *Behavioral Neuroscience, 100*, 147-154.

Thorndike, E. L. (1931). *Human learning.* New York: Century.

Tinbergen, N. (1951). *The study of instinct.* Oxford: Clarendon Press.

Tinkelpaugh, O. L. (1928). An experimental study of representative factors in monkeys. *Journal of Comparative Psychology, 8*, 197-236.

Tolman, E. C. (1932). *Purposive Behavior in Animals and Men.* New York: Century.

Tolman, E. C. (1949). There is more than one kind of learning. *Psychological Review, 56*, 144-155.

Tulving, E. (1972). Episodic and semantic memory. In E. Tulving & W. Donaldson. (Eds.), *Organization of memory.* (pp. 381-403). New York: Academic Press.

Tulving, E., & Schacter, D. L. (1990). Priming and human memory systems. *Science, 247*, 301-306.

Ungerleider, L. G. (1995). Functional brain imaging studies of cortical mechanisms for memory. *Science, 270*, 769-775.

Ungerleider, L. G. & Mishkin, M. (1982). Two cortical visual systems. In D. J. Ingle, M. A. Goodale, & R. J. W. Mansfield. (Eds.), *Analysis of visual behavior.* (pp. 549-586). Cambridge, MA.: MIT Press.

Ungerstedt, U. (1971a). Stereotaxic mapping of the monoamine pathways in the rat brain. *Acta Physiologica Scandinavica, 82* (Suppl 367), 1-48.

Ungerstedt, U. (1971b). Striatal dopamine release after amphetamine or nerve degeneration revealed by rotational behavior. *Acta Physiologica Scandinavica, 82 (Suppl. 367),* 49-68.

Vaccarino, F. J., & Franklin, K. B. J. (1982). Dopamine mediates ipsi- and contraversive circling elicited from the substantia nigra. *Pharmacology Biochemistry and Behavior, 17,* 431-434.

Valenstein, E. S., Cox, V. C., & Kakolewski, J. W. (1968). Modification of motivated behavior elicited by electrical stimulation of the hypothalamus. *Science, 159,* 1119-1121.

Vanderwolf, C. H. (1998). Brain, behavior, and mind: What do we know and what can we know? *Neuroscience and Biobehavioral Review, 22,* 125-142.

Vanderwolf, C. H., & Cain, D. P. (1994). The behavioral neurobiology of learning and memory: A conceptual reorientation. *Brain Research Reviews, 19,* 264-297.

Van Essen, D. C., & Maunsell, J. H. R. (1983). Hierarchical organization and functional streams in the visual cortex. *Trends in Neurosciences, 6,* 370-375.

Van Hoesen, G. W. (1982). The parahippocampal gyrus. *Trends in Neurosciences, 5,* 345-350.

Victor, M., Adams, R. D., & Collins, G. H. (1989). *The Wernicke-Korsakoff syndrome.* (2nd ed.). Philadelphia: F. A. Davis.

von Bonin, G., Garol, H. W., & McCulloch, W. S. (1942). The functional organization of the occipital lobe. In H. Klüver. (Ed.), *Visual mechanisms. Biological symposium,* vol. 7. (pp. 165-192). Lancaster, PA: Cattell Press.

von der Malsburg, C. (1994). The correlation theory of brain function. In E. Domany, J. L. van Hemmen, & K. Schulten. (Eds.), *Models of neural networks II.* (pp. 95-119). New York: Springer-Verlag.

von Senden, M. (1932). *Raum- und Gestaltauffassung bei operierten Blindgeborenen vor und nach der Operation.* Leipzig: Barth.

Waller, W. H. (1940). Progression movements elicited by subthalamic stimulation. *Journal of Neurophysiology, 3,* 300-307.

Walter, W. G. (1953). *The living brain.* New York: W. W. Norton.

Walton, G. E., Bower, N. J., & Bower, T. G. (1992). Recognition of familiar faces by newborns. *Infant Behavior and Development, 15,* 265-269.

Walton, G. E., & Bower, T. G. (1993). Newborns form "prototypes" in less than 1 minute. *Psychological Science, 4,* 203-205.

Warrington, E. K., & Shallice, T. (1969). The selective impairment of auditory verbal short-term memory. *Brain, 92,* 885-896.

Warrington, E. K., & Weiskrantz, L. (1968). A new method of testing long-term retention with special reference to amnesic patients. *Nature, 217,* 972-974.

Warrington, E. K., & Weiskrantz, L. (1970). Amnesic syndrome: Consolidation or retrieval? *Nature, 228,* 628-630.

Watson, J. B. (1919). *Psychology from the standpoint of a behaviorist.* Philadelphia: Lippincott.

Weiskrantz, L. (1990). The Ferrier lecture, 1989. Outlooks for blindsight: Explicit methodologies for implicit processes. *Proceedings of the Royal Society (London) B, 239,* 247-278.

Weiskrantz, L. (1997). *Consciousness lost and found: A neuropsychological exploration.* Oxford: Oxford University Press.

White, N. M. (1986). Control of sensorimotor function by dopaminergic nigrostriatal neurons: Influence on eating and drinking. *Neuroscience and Biobehavioral Review, 10,* 15-36.

White, N. M. (1989). A functional hypothesis concerning the striatal matrix and patches: Mediation of S-R memory and reward. *Life Sciences, 45,* 1943-1957.

White, N. M., & Carr, G. D. (1985). The conditioned place preference is affected by two independent reinforcement processes. *Pharmacology Biochemistry and Behavior, 23,* 37-42.

White, N. M., & Hiroi, N.   (1998). Preferential localization of self-stimulation sites in striosomes/patches in the rat striatum. *Proceedings of the National Academy of Sciences U.S.A.*, *95*, 6486-6491.

White, N. M., & Milner, P. M.   (1992). The psychobiology of reinforcers. *Annual Review of Psychology*, *43*, 443-471.

Williams, M., & Pennybacker, J. (1954). Memory disturbances in third ventricle tumours. *Journal of Neurology, Neurosurgery and Psychiatry*, *17*, 115-123.

Williams, M., & Zangwill, O. L. (1952). Memory defects after head injury. *Journal of Neurology, Neurosurgery and Psychiatry*, *15*, 54-58.

Wilson, M. A., & McNaughton, B. L. (1993). Dynamics of the hippocampal ensemble code for space. *Science*, *261*, 1055-1058.

Winocur, G., Oxbury, S., Roberts, R., Agnetti, V., & Davis, C. (1984). Amnesia in a patient with bilateral lesions to the thalamus. *Neuropsychologia*, *22*, 123-143.

Wise, R. A., & Rompre, P.- P. (1989). Brain dopamine and reward. *Annual Review of Psychology*, *40*, 191-225.

Wise, R. A., Spindler, J., & Legault, L. (1978). Major attenuation of food reward with performance-sparing doses of pimozide in the rat. *Canadian Journal of Psychology*, *32*, 77-85.

Wise, S. P., Boussaoud, D., Johnson, P. B., & Caminiti, R. (1997). Premotor and parietal cortex: Corticocortical connectivity and combinatorial computations. *Annual Review of Neuroscience*, *20*, 25-42.

Wurtz, R. H. (1969). Visual receptive fields of striate cortex neurons in awake monkeys. *Journal of Neurophysiology*, *37*, 727-742.

Yim, C. Y., & Mogenson, G. J. (1988). Neuromodulatory action of dopamine in the nucleus accumbens: An in vivo intracellular study. *Neuroscience*, *26*, 403-415.

Yim, C. Y., & Mogenson, G. J. (1989). Low doses of accumbens dopamine modulate amygdala suppression of spontaneous exploratory activity in rats. *Brain Research*, *477*, 202-210.

Young III, W. S., Bonner, T. I., & Brann, M. R. (1986). Mesencephalic dopamine neurons regulate the expression of neuropeptide mRNAs in the rat forebrain. *Proceedings of the National Academy of Sciences U.S.A.*, *83*, 9827-9831.

Zhuo, M., Kandel, E. R., & Hawkins, R. D. (1994). Nitric oxide and cGMP can produce either synaptic depression or potentiation depending on the frequency of presynaptic stimulation in the hippocampus. *NeuroReport*, *5*, 1033-1036.

Zola-Morgan, S., Squire, L. R., & Amaral, D. G. (1986). Human amnesia and the medial temporal region: Enduring memory impairment following a bilateral lesion limited to field CA1 of the hippocampus. *Journal of Neuroscience*, *6*, 2950-2967.

Zola-Morgan, S., Squire, L. R., Amaral, D. G., & Suzuki, W. (1989). Lesions of perirhinal and parahippocampal cortex that spare the amygdala and hippocampal formation produce severe memory impairment. *Journal of Neuroscience*, *9*, 4355-4370.

Zubin, J., & Barrera, S. E. (1941). Effect of electric convulsive therapy on memory. *Proceedings of the Society for Experimental Biology and Medicine*, *48*, 596-597.

Author Index

Subject Index